# The Commander's Invitation

Experiencing Manifestation in Prayer

## Dr. David E. Jackson

# THE COMMANDER'S INVITATION

### Experiencing Manifestation in Prayer

## DR. DAVID E. JACKSON

Lithonia, GA

© 2020 David E. Jackson
All rights reserved.

No part of this publication may be reproduced, stored in a retrieval system or transmitted in any form or by any means, electronic, mechanical, photocopying, recording or otherwise, without the expressed written permission of the publisher.

Scripture references are taken primarily from the King James Version of the Holy Bible; other versions are also used. Pronouns for referring to the Father, Son and Holy Spirit are capitalized intentionally and the words satan and devil are never capitalized.

Publisher:
MEWE, LLC
www.mewellc.com

First Edition
ISBN: 978-1-7334383-5-3

Library of Congress Control Number: 2019921207

Printed in the United States of America.

*I dedicate this book to the faithful men and women who commit to praying with me for manifestation every week on social media.*

# TABLE OF CONTENTS

Introduction ................................................................. ix

Chapter 1: A Theology of Commanding Your Morning ......... 1

Chapter 2: The 3 Ms of Manifestation ................................. 13

Chapter 3: Mindset for Manifestation ................................. 19

Chapter 4: The Mouth: The Gateway to Reality ................. 41

Chapter 5: The Mechanics of Manifestation ....................... 59

Appendix: 5 Days of Commanding Your Morning .............. 77

    Day One: Four Winds ................................................. 78

    Day Two: Prayers of Protection ................................. 83

    Day Three: The Breaker's Anointing ......................... 88

    Day Four: Rebuking the Spirit of Pisgah ................... 92

    Day Five: The Commander's Prayer .......................... 96

About the Author ............................................................. 103

# INTRODUCTION

I was in the airport on my way back home a couple of years ago and the phrase "Command your Morning" dropped into my spirit. Thanks to the ministry of Dr. Cindy Trimm, I was familiar with the importance of starting my day with declarations and decrees. However, I did not have a consistent prayer life, to be honest. I would say a few things to God here and there, but I was not fully devoted to praying in the spirit and in my native language on a daily basis. I knew that it was important to declare and decree and that I could bind and loose based on what the Bible said. However, I neglected these powerful actions for more sleep, checking my social media, or rushing to start my day.

After hearing "Command Your Morning" in my spirit, I felt a strong mandate to begin to teach this principle to my congregation and started investigating the matter. I listened to several videos on the topic and, the more I watched, the more my interest was piqued. I then found key information from Dr. Daniel Olukoya from Nigeria and his seminal book, *Command the Morning* and other powerful prayer books. I was reintroduced to a concept that I learned from my ministry work in Ghana, West Africa, and that was using prayer points when I prayed. Prayer points are pre-written statements, declarations, and requests that have been collected around specific topics such as healing, breakthroughs, relationships, and finances. It seemed strange to me as first that I would read prayers from a book. However, I quickly discovered that getting results in prayer is not about simply praying. It is about being specific and laser sharp in your requests. I went to the scriptures to see what was there about this topic. Results in prayer also require us to be keenly aware of when and what may be hindering the manifestation of requests from God.

My study started initially with the only scripture in the Bible that says, "Command the morning." That passage is found in the book of Job:

> *Have you commanded the morning since your days began, And caused the dawn to know its place...?* ( Job 38:12)

God's question to Job came in the form of a challenge when he questioned the trials he was facing. When I first read Job 38:12 and started reading and listening to videos, I did believe we had the right to command the morning; however, there were some gaps in the biblical support for such a practice. I needed a stronger biblical theology to support this authoritative act in prayer. As I continued to do more research and pray, I realized that God was not only challenging Job's questioning, but He was also giving Job a divine invitation to become a commander of his day and life. This happens when one opens their mouth and declares what they want to see in their day and what they refuse to experience. This activity takes place early in the morning and can chart the course of the entire day. The word "commander" jumped out at me because of my law enforcement background.

What is a commander? A commander is a person who has been given the right or authority over a situation, group of people, or territory. A commander is a leader and a member of a high class or order. As a child of God and an ambassador of Christ, you have been authorized by the Holy Spirit inside of you to dominate your day, your sector of the marketplace, your community, and your reality. The commander's invitation is a kingdom mandate to arise and ascend from an Earth-bound posture and mentality in prayer and declaration to your rightful place, which is in the heavenly places. Ephesians 2:6 assures us that we have been seated (signifies authority) in the heavenly realms (the third Heaven) with Christ because we have been raised up with Him through our faith in Him as our Savior.

Just as God issued Job this invitation, God has given every believer a Commander's Invitation to a lifestyle of taking authority over your day and life. Becoming a daily commander requires an understanding of the connection between declarations, decrees, spiritual knowledge, posture, and manifestation in terms of getting consistent results in prayer.

The purpose of this book is to share with you some of the research, revelations, and biblical principles that authorize you to be a commander in prayer. This book was birthed out of a mandate from God to provide a strong biblical framework for commanding the morning. God showed me that He is the God of manifestation and we His people should also be walking in a higher level of manifestation. There are five chapters in this book.

Chapter 1 is entitled "A Theology of Commanding Your Morning." In chapter 1, I will attempt to build a biblical and theological framework for why you have the authority to command your morning. In all of your getting, you want to get understanding. Gaining knowledge will help to minimize missing the target in prayer and thereby not getting results.

Chapter 2 is a brief introduction into the meat of this book, "The 3Ms of Manifestation." At the time I started studying and teaching this revelation, I was in transition in my life. I realized that my increased efforts in prayer and fasting were still not producing results in my life. Then I learned about the spirit of Pisgah from Dr. Olukoya and how it is a tricky spirit that brings you to the edge of your promise but then blocks you from crossing over to possess it. We see the story of Moses in Mt. Nebo at the pinnacle (Pisgah) at the border of the Promised Land in Deuteronomy 34:1. The 3Ms are designed to help you battle the spirit of Pisgah and other spiritual forces that prevent manifestation in your prayer life.

Chapter 3 is entitled "Mindset of Manifestation." This chapter will address the important role that our thoughts play in getting results in prayer. Proverbs 23:7 lets us know that as a man thinks in his/her heart, so is he/she. Are your thoughts hindering you from getting what you are believing God for? This section will help you take inventory of your thought life, and make the necessary adjustments to experience results in prayer.

Chapter 4 is called "The Mouth: The Gateway to Reality." Matthew 12:34 says, out of the heart, the mouth speaks. Your thoughts become words and the words that come out of your mouth become your reality. Hebrews 11:3 helps us understand that by faith the worlds were framed at the command or by the words of God. This fact connects to the next chapter.

Chapter 5 is "The Mechanics of Manifestation." In order to experience consistent results in prayer, one must understand the inner workings of manifestation. Otherwise, your results will be hit and miss. You will not be able to explain why you experience manifestation. This chapter will dissect the inner components of manifestation and show how each aspect connects to ultimately produce results.

A key concept to understanding manifestation is knowing who God really is. For instance, the Hebrew word for God is *Elohim*, which speaks of the creative nature of God. This is the One who can take nothing and make something. Then He can take what He made and make it into something else. Elohim created everything in the Creation narrative in Genesis with His words – except for Adam. We are made in the image of God based on Genesis 1:27. This means we also have the power to create with our words. This section will give you insight and knowledge that will empower you to see repeated manifestation in your life.

At the end of the book, you will find the Appendix called "5 Days of Commanding Your Morning." As I shared at the beginning, using prayer points is a powerful tool to help you in your prayer life. I have provided 5 days of specific prayer points to use. I have also included scriptures or devotional reading, times of praying in the spirit or praising God (if you do not have a prayer language), and times of silence/laying prostrate to hear from God. I pray that these targeted prayers bring abundant manifestation in your life. My heart for the readers of this book is that your reality shifts from missing the target in your prayer life because you either are unaware of the authority you have or you lack the proper knowledge. James 4:3 suggests that one of the reasons some people do not get answers to prayer is because they ask amiss. Amiss means our prayers are not exactly right, inappropriate or out of place. As a result, we do not experience the manifestation of what we have prayed for. We need assistance in knowing how and what to pray for.

Further, we must remember that prayer and manifestation is as much a spiritual matter as it is a natural one. There is a constant spiritual battle going on between God and the enemy and, at times, we are caught in the middle of it. Therefore, we have to know the proper tools and weapons to defeat our opponent through Christ's power. However, we cannot know what weapons to use unless we know the enemy we are fighting. 2 Corinthians 10:4 tells us that the weapons of our warfare are not carnal but mighty through God to the pulling down of strongholds!

All of this and more is awaiting you in *The Commander's Invitation*. I am excited to take this journey with you, Commander! You will not regret accepting this divine invitation from the Most High God to shift into a reality of authority, effectiveness, and manifestation in your life.

Dr. David E. Jackson

# CHAPTER 1

A THEOLOGY OF
COMMANDING YOUR MORNING

Dr. Olukoya's book on commanding the morning shifted my life as it began to deal with an aspect of prayer and spiritual warfare that many Christians have not been taught or have rejected as being demonic or associated with witchcraft. This concept is based on understanding how to pray and legislate from the spiritual and cosmological realms. We as Christians have the authority in Jesus' name to speak to our sun, moon, and stars with the understanding that there are demonic forces working against us in that realm to block, misalign, and hinder things that God has already released to His people. Two important scriptures to remember when talking about the cosmological realm are Psalm 121:5-6 and Ephesians 6:12:

*The LORD watches over you— the LORD is your shade at your right hand; the sun will not harm you by day, nor the moon by night* (Psalm 121:5-6).

*For we do not wrestle against flesh and blood, but against principalities, against powers, against the rulers of the darkness of this age, against spiritual hosts of wickedness in the heavenly places* (Ephesians 6:12).

Psalm 121 suggests that you can be hindered in the cosmos (i.e. sun, moon, stars) if you do not declare protection. The preceding verse states that the LORD (Jehovah/Yahweh) is the keeper. The word for keeper in the Hebrew is *shamar*, which means helper, watchman, and protector. So, the key to legislating in the cosmos is to enlist the watchman aspect of the self-existing, promise-making, covenant-keeping God of Israel. Ephesians 6 shows us that the source of our opposition is not natural or human, but spiritual. There are different ranks of spiritual forces and they all reside in the Heavenlies, more specifically, the second Heaven.

Another essential passage to consider in this discussion is in Daniel 10:12-14:

*Then he said to me, "Do not fear, Daniel, for from the first day that you set your heart to understand, and to humble yourself before your God, your words were heard; and I have come because of your words. But the prince of the kingdom of Persia withstood me twenty-one days; and behold, Michael, one of the chief princes, came to help me, for I had been left alone there with the kings of Persia. Now I have come to make you understand what will happen to your people in the latter days, for the vision refers to many days yet to come."*

In this passage, Daniel prayed to God for an answer concerning the Jewish people's condition in exile. Daniel sensed that there was an unusual delay in hearing from God and decided to fast until the answer came to him. This lasted for about 21 days (what many people call the Daniel Fast). On the 21$^{st}$ day, Daniel had an angelic visitation. Partnering with and activating angels is another key component to getting manifestation in prayer. The angel, who is a messenger of God, revealed to Daniel that the day he set his heart to understand and humble himself before God, was the day his words were heard, and the answer was released. However, the manifestation of the answer was delayed by the demonic principality of the Persian Empire (keep Ephesians 6:12 in mind). As a result, the archangel of warfare, Michael, was released to help this angel so that he could be freed to bring the answer to Daniel. There is a powerful revelation in this story about prayer, fasting, spiritual warfare, and manifestation. Commanding the morning is an act of spiritual warfare that directly addresses any demonic or opposing forces to the manifestation of your prayers or the direction of your day.

Why is there demonic opposition to your prayers? Because God fulfilling your prayers helps to advance the overall Kingdom agenda. Do you know why the devil fights the Kingdom? Because that's exactly what Jesus preached. The devil is anti-Christ, meaning he is against Him. Anything that Christ is for, he is against. That's why he fights marriages. That's why he fights unity. That's why he fights the church because Christ is for all of them. And, above all, the devil fights the word of God because it is Jesus Christ Himself.

In the Bible, God challenges Job with this amazing question:

> *Have you commanded the morning since your days began and caused the dawn to know his place?* (Job 38:12)

I will put the same question to you. How have you been doing in terms of commanding the morning? Commanding your morning is simply a practice where you get up early between the hours of 4:00 am and 6:00 am ideally. You can still wake up at 7:00 am or 8:00 am and still command. But the goal is to get up as early as possible to have a head start before your day begins.

One of the reasons is because witches and warlocks pray during the 3rd Prayer Watch (12:00AM to 3:00AM), also known as the Witching Hours. What are prayer watches? These are three-hour blocks (eight watches total) of time where specific prayers and activities take place. In the Bible, there were no camera or alarm systems to alert cities that danger was approaching. Rather, faithful men would take shifts or watches standing on the city walls. Today, we, as prayer warriors, are called to stand on the walls for our families, churches, and communities watching for both the enemy's work to block it as well as for the manifestation of God's plans. Can you guess when the Commanding Hours are? Right after the Witching ones, the 4th Prayer Watch (3:00 AM to 6:00 AM). The 4th Watch is a strategic time in prayer as it is the last one of the night season. It is also an important time because you get an opportunity to counteract and reverse the works of the enemy! There is a key scripture to keep in mind about prayer watches in St. Matthew 24:43 that reads, *"But know this, that if the goodman of the house had known in what watch the thief would come, he would have watched, and would not have suffered his house to be broken up."*

**Commander! God is inviting you to become more aware of when the enemy, who is the thief, is trying to wreak havoc on your house.**

You get up and you start declaring and decreeing. To declare means to speak with seriousness and boldness. Get serious and bold in your statements. How do you acquire that boldness? It comes from the Holy Spirit empowerment. It also comes when you know who you are: a son of the Most High God. The Bible says we are all sons – it does not have anything to do with gender. The notion of sonship is a spiritual one. Say to yourself, *I am a son. And. because I am a son, I have an intimate relationship with God. I have the right to speak to Him, not tremble before Him.*

Imagine if your child was hesitant to come to you if you've been a good parent? Then there is no reason to be hesitant in coming before our Father in prayer (See Matthew 7:9-11). Move in confidence versus fear when you go to God. So, you go before God in the morning and make your declarations, which means you are serious and you're bold. You are making specific statements about how your day is going to go. When you decree something, you are making a legal statement. You are not speaking in your own voice; you are speaking out of the authority that comes from relationship with Jesus.

**Binding and Loosing**

Again, God gives you the tools to declare what will happen and what will not happen. They are binding and loosing:

*"Truly I say to you, whatever you bind on earth shall have been bound in heaven and whatever you loose on earth, shall have been loosed in heaven"* (Matthew 18:18 NASB).

Do you know the impact of binding and loosing? To bind means to forbid: "I forbid this from happening! I bind the spirit of strife in my workplace." Tell yourself, "I have the power to forbid. I have the authority in the name of Jesus to forbid evil from happening. I'm exercising my authority and that wickedness has to stop today, not tomorrow, not next week, but today. Some trouble is ending today. It's over and done with. You are not going into my week. You are not going into next year with me. I bind you." Remember this: some bad things still may happen but, when you get into the practice of doing it every single day, its hold begins to weaken.

God said, "Before you even speak it, I've already done it," meaning, "I heard it on your mind." You get to a place where God partners with your thoughts. You don't just want to back them up with His word, you want to partner with His thoughts. Before God even comes up in your mind, you are already thinking His thoughts. Just as binding is to forbidding, loosing is permitting. When you loose, you release or unlock something such as "I loose the blessing of the Lord over my neighborhood." Have you ever felt that there was something that was holding up your blessing? Did you ever sense an invisible force acting behind the scenes? So when you get up in the morning, know that you have the power to forbid that thing from holding up your blessing. Be confident because Heaven is backing you up, ready to support what you seek. That means, when you open your mouth, your worries are going to fall to the ground. When your worries are cast down, your blessings begin to surface. You're going to reap what is due to you; it's going to manifest in your life.

**All Heaven Declares**

For those of you who feel that you are alone and no one is there for you, I want you to know that all Heaven is with you. Your friends may not be with you but, when you open your mouth, all of the host of Heaven is standing behind your words. If heaven is standing behind the words, no demon from hell, in hell, through hell, can block what you're saying. Heaven is backing your statements and no weapon against your declarations can prosper and can stand against them. Summon up that confidence in your spirit that nothing can stand against Heaven.

You are declaring and you are decreeing in the morning. Not only are you exerting your rights as sons but you have also been called to partner with God. Now declare and decree that you will no longer just be an observer of life, taking in what comes and goes; you are about to become a participant in your life. You are about to become the orchestrator of your life. You can rewrite your reality.

Open your mouth and declare and decree what God is expecting you to take charge of – your spiritual growth, your household, your nation, as examples. Too many Christians are just experiencing and accepting what life brings. But know that

God has transitioned you by faith to open your mouth and to begin to declare before daybreak what this day will be, what this day will bring and what the devil is not going to do.

The reason why the devil is active in your life is because you did not bind him before he could aim his weapons at you. Say, "Before you get started, devil, I call everything you plan to happen today to fall to the ground void. I declare and decree that it will not happen in my life. It will not happen to my spouse, it will not happen to my children."

Isaiah 30:15 says, *"In quietness and confidence shall be your strength."* When you get up early in the morning, it's very quiet and still. You feel it's almost unreal, like time is frozen. But God said, "In those times you will receive My strength." Before the day starts, before the e-mails break in, before the text messages roll in, before the drama gets plays out, He gives us His strength...but we have to seek Him early in the morning (See Psalm 63:1). How you start your day will determine how the rest of the day will go. It's easier to start with the right frame of mind than to get up later struggling to get your mind right.

Whether or not you command your body, the day has already been planned for you. What I'm challenging you to do is to say, "Whatever the day has planned for me that is not in alignment with the will of God, will not be so." You have to do it early, while it's still quiet and still because God promises to meet with you early and give you His strength.

As a believer, you receive good preaching every week but you may not apply everything you hear. Many days you get up with the devil sitting inside your head and giving you a litany of bad news. It's time to make your Sunday mornings the place to equip you for the week. Tell yourself, "Every day I am victorious." It all starts with changing your speech.

## Job Versus Traditional Theology

I now want to talk about traditional theology with particular reference to Job 1. Job was a righteous man, a wealthy businessman of good social standing. One day satan has a conversation in Heaven with God in which satan questions the integrity of Job's relationship with God, claiming that the only reason that Job praises God is because he is so blessed. God maintains that Job is a good and upright man, and even if Job goes through the storm, he will still praise Him. So, the devil has permission to launch his attack on the man (See Job 1:8-12).

That's what the devil is really doing when you're attacked. Don't miss this. The devil is not attacking you to stop you from fulfilling your destiny. Your destiny is already set. The devil can't stop this. What he's trying to do is to frustrate the in-between phase to the point that, when you hear God, you are so defeated that you can't appreciate Him. The only reason you won't get to your destiny is, if in your trouble, you curse God. Satan wants you to blaspheme. He wants you to begin to say that God isn't who He says He is, and that in the middle of difficulties, God is a liar. That's the devil's plan for you.

Remember that the devil didn't start out in hell. Hell was created for him when he rebelled against God. He thought that he could set himself against God, but he lost. Even so, the devil knows the way to get back at God is if he can get covenant people to call God a liar.

The devil constantly brings up accusations before God, for instance, that your praise, your worship, your lifting up of hands, your offerings and your service are not genuine. They are only in response to the good things and protection He provides.

So, Job becomes the target of the devil. God gives him permission to go and touch him but not to touch his soul. The devil can touch your finances, he can touch your job, he can touch your relationships, but he can't touch your soul.

So, the devil launches his attacks on Job. He kills all his children in one day. All of his business goes in one day. But Job says that the Lord gives, the Lord takes away (See Job 1:21).

Well, satan comes back and reassesses his position, "I thought it was these things that made him praise You and call You Lord. Let me give him some more."

The second layer after your possessions is your image. Since satan did not find any success in touching Job's possessions, he sets his sights on attacking Job's image. He attacks his body." When we go through sickness, it's not just a matter of health, it concerns our image. The devil attacks us sometimes in our health, to undermine our confidence and how we present ourselves to people. He hopes that we will begin to curse God and blame him from impacting our image.

You can't hide sickness. Everybody can see that; everybody will have something to say "Why is he sick? What did he do? How is she dealing with it?"

And so, the devil says, "I'm going to impact Job's image. I bet he's going to curse God after this." So, the devil touched Job by giving him open sores all over his body. To make matters worse, his friends came to see him in this state and loaded him with their theology.

Job did not realize this, but God was positioning him to break the traditional mold of the day. This theology reasons that because God is almighty, when He deals with you, it is the result of some sin you have committed. Because you have committed some sin or done some evil, God will punish you in front of people.

As good as tradition is, tradition is not always right. Remember this: every rule has an exception, but the exception reinforces the rule. Things may happen but not everything is always as it appears.

God was positioning Job to break such a tradition. He was going to use Job by publicly putting him through this great trial. People would assume that it was because of sin but God was about to show them how wrong they were.

If there's something that you're going through, that is not necessarily because you are evil but because you are righteous. God may be using you to break that traditional mindset. He knows that people will have a whole lot to say about your condition, without an iota of understanding into the heart of the matter. Whatever people may speculate, as long God knows the truth, you can face it. You've been built to go through this, and God gives you the grace. God will use you, like Job, as the exception to prove that you can be righteous and still go through severe testing.

So, Job had to endure the accusations of his friends who insisted he had done some terrible thing to merit such a punishment. Hearing all of this, Job almost gave way to tradition and almost admitted he had done something. Under all the weight of his situation, he was almost about to charge God foolishly. He had held up his faith as long as he could and now was at breaking point. And this is the moment that God spoke. Job confessed, "I believe You, God; I trust You. But I can't handle these people and their taunts in my ear and in my mind. I've had it!"

You've been holding up your faith as long as you could. You're at the point where you just can't take it anymore. It's also at your breaking point that God will speak. He is getting ready to have a conversation with you. God is not going to let you break.

Now God begins to challenge Job for questioning His integrity. Basically, God is defending His supremacy, His sovereignty, His provision, His might.

"Have you commanded the mornings since your days began? God asks Job, "Have you ever set out the course of your days since you were born?" (See Job 38:12)

"No," says Job.

"Well, I've done that for you."

**Counter Culture**

Underlying the notion of commanding his morning was God challenging Job not to give in to tradition. You see, commanding your morning is countercultural. Another way of saying countercultural is "Kingdom business." Because the Kingdom is God's culture, to command your morning is, in effect, to say, "Thy Kingdom come..." In other words, you are enforcing God's design and His plan in your life.

What gives us the authority to command our morning?

Anytime you look at scripture, you see God showing us something that He does. That gives you a glimpse into what you, too, can do. He is saying that anything He does in the scriptures gives you a foretaste of what you have the authority to do. What gives you the authority to do it? The fact that you are made in His image and likeness. So the same thing that you see God say He does in the scriptures, if you can tap into your faith, is also your right.

If God asks Job if he commanded his morning, it is also an invitation to Job to set out to command it. Sometimes the challenges of God are invitations to rise up to a new dimension of enforcing His will. This is God's invitation to you today. God has the power to give His words creative force. Since you are made in the image of God, you have the same creative power to command your morning.

What challenges do you have right now that you are complaining about? See God's challenge to command your morning as an actual invitation from God. He is challenging you: "What do you want to do about it? Are you going to react foolishly? Or are you going to take authority with your mouth and begin to command what will be and what will not be?"

There are three Ms to command your morning: your Mind, your Mouth and your Manifestation. The reason why some of you are struggling with what you say is because your mentality has to shift. You speak out of the abundance of your heart. Whatever comes up in your heart and whatever you feel is what you speak. If your heart and mind are not lining up with the word of God, then you've got to fight with your mind against the day's challenges. You've got to make your mind submit to the word by faith and by an act of will.

# CHAPTER 2

## THE 3 MS OF MANIFESTATION

A few years ago, I was in an intense season of transition in my career and personal life. I became more committed to my personal time with the Lord. I was consistent every day in prayer, reading the Bible, and worship. I would on occasion add days of fasting to support my petitions for a successful crossover to the promises of God for the next season of life. With all of these efforts, I was still not seeing the manifestation to all of my prayers on a consistent basis. I begin to seek the Lord for insight and answers. God directed me to begin to study the connection between prayer and manifestation. I realized upon deeper study that manifestation is a crucial aspect of being a Commander because what is the point of praying, declaring, and decreeing and you never see results from your words?

**Why Manifestation Is Important**

What exactly is manifestation? Manifestation is the embodiment of an abstract idea, concept or principle. It is when an invisible abstract idea becomes tangible and you can touch and see it. Manifestation is also a transition from the invisible to the visible.

Manifestation is a public demonstration of power and purpose. Allow me to take the definition of manifestation to a deeper level spiritually. Everything that exists first starts in the invisible, spiritual world. It is created by the words of someone, be it a human or supernatural being. When that thing moves into the visible natural world, then we can see it materialize. The process of moving from the supernatural realm to the natural is the manifestation.

Why is this important to understand manifestation in terms of getting results in prayer? One reason is that you must have confidence that when you pray in accordance with the will of God for something, that He hears you and releases the answer in the invisible, spiritual realm. When you discern or detect that what you prayed for is unusually delayed, it is not proper to assume that God is not answering. Rather, you should immediately think, "What force or reality is blocking the manifestation or transfer or my answer from the invisible to the visible world?" Also, the delay may be about the proper timing for manifestation.

**Roadblocks to Manifestation**

What are some of the forces or situations that can hinder the shift of answered prayers from the spirit world to the natural world?

- Demonic forces and opposition to the shift
- Lack of focus and specificity in prayer
- Unrepentance in our hearts and lives
- Not using the right weapon/tool based on the situation and opponent

As I started seeking God for why I was not seeing results, He told me that many people pray and ask for things without knowledge of the three Ms of Manifestation. The three Ms of Manifestation are:

- Mindset for Manifestation
- The Mouth: The Gateway to Reality
- The Mechanics of Manifestation

This revelation has shifted my entire life and caused me to experience consistent manifestation in my life. In the next three chapters, allow me to share these power insights with you.

# CHAPTER 3

MINDSET FOR MANIFESTATION

First, we will deal with your mind. In the book of Proverbs, it says, *"For as he thinks in his heart, so is he"* (Proverbs 23:7). That is to say, the substance of one's being is not external but internal. In other words, you can dress up, fix up, and do whatever you want to decorate and make your outer being look beautiful but the crux of the matter is that you are really what you think in your heart. In the Bible, when you see the word "heart," it not only refers to the physical organ that pumps blood in your system. It also refers to your inner being, the center and core of who you are. It is this heart that houses your emotions, will, and intellect. Your heart, used in this context, is figurative.

Proverbs 23:7 also suggests that our internal lives can differ significantly from our external lives. What people show you on the outside may not be who they really are on the inside. The truth of the matter is that, if you really want to discover who a person really is, you have to find out who they are on the inside, not the outside. Hence, the adage: "Don't judge a book by its cover."

In fact, people do a good job of pretending. Therefore, the Bible says not to trust what you see on the outside if what is on the inside does not match. No wonder God told Samuel, concerning His selection of the next King of Israel, that He is not moved by our outward appearances. Rather, He looks at the hearts of men (See I Samuel 16:7). If our outward actions do not match our hearts, we are insincere and untruthful.

Proverbs 23:7 gives words of wisdom pertaining to those who pretend to be our friends when, in fact, they are our enemies. *"Eat and drink, saith he to thee; but his heart is not with thee"* (Proverbs 23:7 KJV). This is a major concern for any of us because sometimes, people are so good at masking their true feelings, we can be deceived and unable to discern the truth. It is not difficult to understand this scenario. As a matter of fact, it happens every day. People can encourage us with enthusiasm and make us feel they are cheering us on, when, in fact, they are jealous and threatened by our endeavors. Like the person in this verse, they may appear to rejoice with you but, on the inside, they are not on your side.

It is important to make sure that, when you are interacting with people, and more importantly, with yourself, your outward appearance, expressions, words, and actions are congruent with who you are on the inside. Don't be the kind of person who says one thing and means something else on the inside.

Now, you may ask, "What connection does mindset have with manifestation?" Remember, commanding your morning is all about the words you speak in faith. Your faith expects that the words you declare and decree will cause your requests to move from the spiritual realm into the physical, earthly realm: that is the manifestation.

Manifestation means that what is invisible in the spirit realm becomes visible in the earthly realm. That happens because your words are released into the atmosphere by faith for something to happen. What is the link then between your mindset and the manifestation? The link is your words. However, before you can really deal with your words, you have to address your thoughts. You have to deal with the way you think. Our words test us. They do not start in our mouths; they start in our hearts. That's the Kingdom nugget that you want to remember.

**What's in Your Heart?**

*"The intrinsically good man..."* begins Luke 6:45. What does "intrinsically" mean? It is what comes naturally and easily

to a person on the inside or the natural state of a person's inner being. The intrinsically good man produces what is good, honorable, and moral out of the good treasures stored in his heart. On the other hand, the intrinsically evil man produces what is wicked and depraved out of the evil in his heart, *"for his mouth speaks from the overflow of his heart"* (Luke 6:45 AMPC). In some versions of the Bible, this verse is also translated *"out of the abundance of the heart, the mouth speaks."*

If you have goodness in your heart, inevitably, the overflow of that goodness will determine your words. But if you are naturally an evil person in your heart, then your words will be evil, slanderous and profane.

Jesus echoes these thoughts when He speaks to the Pharisees saying: *"O generation of vipers, how can ye, being evil, speak good things? For out of the abundance of the heart the mouth speaketh"* (Matthew 12:34). Jesus was telling the religious leaders that they could only produce what was in their hearts. How could their words be good when their hearts were not? For out of the abundance of the heart, the mouth speaks.

If you are honest and sincere with your words, you do so because in your heart, you are honest and sincere. On the other hand, if you are a person who constantly speaks evil, it is an indicator that your heart is evil. In other words, your conversations reveal the condition of your heart. That is so powerful.

It stands to reason, therefore, that if you really want to know who a person is, it may be worth listening to what they say. This is where we discern the spirit of a person. We hear the conversations. We hear the words. We can feel the spirit, energy or vibes, but we know that it doesn't match up with who we think they are or how they want to be perceived. Consequently, we often ignore or disregard our feelings or what we are discerning, rather than give it its due recognition.

If you say you are a nice person, yet every word that comes out of your mouth is negative or gossip and talking evil about people, there is a disconnect. It doesn't matter how good you say you are or intend to be, the condition of your heart is not good.

It follows that you have to be careful that you're not looking for good in people who are inherently evil. Why? You will sacrifice yourself and your peace of mind trying to redeem them. Now, it is one thing to stand with a person who has a good heart but is in a bad condition but to sacrifice yourself for someone who is naturally evil is foolhardy.

Here are some Bible verses you may want to consider: *"Keep thy heart with all diligence, for out of it are the issues of life"* (Proverbs 4:23). This verse clearly teaches us to protect our hearts. You have to be serious and dedicated to this. You have to fight to keep your heart pure because if you don't, the spring of life that flows from it will be contaminated.

*"The mouth of the righteous is a well of life, But violence covers the mouth of the wicked"* (Proverbs 10:11). People who are righteous in their hearts produce words like a fountain of life. Their speech is like water, which flows and brings life. But the mouth of those who are wicked, it conceals. Conceal means to hide violence, which suggests that they are setting you up for a violent attack, but they have hidden it from you until it's too late to know that danger is upon you.

*"Every way of a man is right in his own eyes, But the Lord weighs the hearts"* (Proverbs 12:2). This verse says that a person can have an evil heart and not be aware of it. They

think their words and their actions are right. But God truly knows the intentions and the motives behind people's actions. He weighs them out. Or you can say, He checks and balances the hearts, the motives, and the intentions of people.

**Managing Your Heart Condition**

In short, the key to real manifestation in your life is learning how to maintain a heart or a mindset that produces good and not evil. Even after salvation you have to make sure that your heart doesn't become contaminated, for you received a brand new heart when you were saved.

The Bible says that God takes out our stony hearts and replaces them with hearts of flesh that can love and be pliable (See Ezekiel 36:28). Having a heart of flesh does not mean you are simple minded. Rather, you are a person that is sensitive and receptive to God. You have to protect your heart, intellect, emotions, and will to make sure that the issues of life, the struggles, the hard things you see and experience do not contaminate your heart to the point where you become, bitter, resentful, and unforgiving.

You cannot expect to receive anything from God if your language is evil, negative, full of gossip and lies and if you engage in raunchy conversations. These things do not reflect a good heart. How can you expect to receive the manifestation of the promises of God with such language?

To be honest with you, I know that managing and protecting your heart and your mind is much easier said than done. This is so because the mind is a battlefield. It is there that the enemy chooses to create the fiercest battles between good and evil. Why? Because what's happening in your mind is directly connected to what's happening in your life. If you want to understand what's going on in your life, examine your thoughts. What do you think about? What emotions are you feeling? Where is your will in relationship to its alignment or misalignment to the will of God? The answers to these questions will give you an indication of what's happening in your life because what's happening in your mind will come out in what you say. And what you say is what you will see and have. Your language is the gateway to your reality.

Sometimes, it's a daily fight to win the battle in our minds but you have to stand your ground and put on the whole armor of God (See Ephesians 6:10-18). Part of winning on the battlefield of the mind is allowing the Holy Spirit inside of you to wage warfare by praying in the Spirit. How often do you pray in the Spirit? Do you take time every day to pray in the Holy Ghost? You see, when you pray in the Holy Ghost, you build up yourself on the inside (See Jude 20). You are waging war in your mind against the thoughts, ideas, feelings, and elements of your will that are contrary to God.

If you are not praying in the Holy Ghost regularly then you're not equipping yourself to fight on the battlefield. If you claim the Word of God is your sword, which is your offensive weapon, but you're not using it and if you are not reading, applying, and meditating on the Word regularly in your mind and heart, then you're not really equipping yourself to win the war in your mind.

Jesus said that faith is our shield, so if you're not using faith as your shield, you have nothing to protect you from the relentless fire of the enemy. You have no way of combating the words, images, feelings, and experiences that are the fiery darts the enemy shoots at you. Without your faith being intact, you are fully exposed to danger. While you may have the breastplate of righteousness, you will find it is constantly under attack. Hence, your salvation is constantly being challenged because the concept of salvation is in your head. Imagine the enemy trying to get past your shield of faith so he can assault your righteousness and your salvation. He's trying to bombard your mind to convince you that you're not saved and assail your heart so that you forget that you are the righteousness of God in Christ.

You have to keep your faith intact, keep it up to block those fiery missiles. Use the Word of God to chop down those things that come to destroy you, those assailants that come to slaughter you. Your mouth has to be a part of your defense. It is just as much a part of the armor as any of the other pieces. What does your mouth do? It prays in the Holy Ghost.

**Conforming to Which Culture?**

A mindset of manifestation, therefore, is a mind whose battles lead you to victory on the side of good and God's will. That's what you want. You need daily renewal. Again, these are tools for a mindset that leads to manifestation. This is absolutely essential as you command your morning.

> *I beseech you therefore, brethren, by the mercies of God, that you present your bodies a living sacrifice, holy, acceptable to God, which is your reasonable service. And do not be conformed to this world, but be transformed by the renewing of your mind, that you may prove what is that good and acceptable and perfect will of God* (Romans 12:1-2).

To understand the word "conform" in this context, I want you to imagine a cake pan. I'm not sure about you but when I was growing up, my grandma used to bake cakes from scratch. She would mix up the ingredients and grease the cake pans. It was amazing because she had differently-shaped cake pans, some circular, some square, while some had ridges. When my grandma took that batter and poured it into the cake pan, the batter would take on the shape of the pan. On completion, when the cake was taken out of the pan, it would be the same shape of the pan. The batter conformed to the pan.

Conforming is a shaping word; it is about taking the shape of something. Paul is saying don't be shaped into the way the world thinks. There is a Kingdom way of thinking that is different from the world's way of thinking. The Kingdom way of thinking is countercultural, against the prevailing culture. Don't let the world force you to fit into their mold or patterns of thinking.

Whatever the prevailing culture is saying, more than likely, the Kingdom is saying the opposite. The culture may say there is no need for marriage and marriage doesn't work. However, the Kingdom says marriage is still honorable in the eyes of God. The culture says that it's okay to mix things together that don't fit but the Kingdom voice still says there is a distinction between good and evil, right and wrong. There is still a difference between unclean and clean. Holiness is still the standard in the Kingdom culture regardless of society's shifting values.

As believers, you have to make a daily decision not to conform to the mold that the world wants to fit you into. How do they fit you in? They, subtly and many times openly, use media (radio, TV, Internet, social media, etc.), music, fashion, and culture to inject their values into you. You have to pay attention to what's driving the world's culture. It's not God; but, rather, it's the god of this world. The culture is influenced by evil. It's time for the godly people in the world to dominate the marketplace to have a stronger voice and be more influential in our society.

The powers that be and other cultural movements have no interest in putting forth a godly Kingdom worldview. You have to be very careful and discerning when you're taking in information and ideas that you are not supporting something contrary to God's will. For example, you may not necessarily be a trendy dresser but you do like to look at things. You should ask yourself, "What is the real spirit behind some of the fashion that you're seeing?" Make sure that you're not embracing a fashion or doing something with your dress that is not in line with the Kingdom perspective.

Paul goes on to say that to avoid being poured into the world's mold of thought, you have to be transformed by the renewing of your mind. This is how you break the world's influence on your mind or how you prevent yourself from being poured like batter into the world's cake pan so to speak.

The word "to renew" (*anakainoó* in Greek) suggests a renovation. You have to renovate your mind. When you renovate something, you take it from its original state and transform it into something completely different.

Usually, after renovation, the project looks nothing like the old one. Let's say you want to renovate your bathroom or your kitchen. You want to change the color of the walls; you want to change the tiles or the shelves. You go in, tear down everything that's in the way and you put in something completely new. Likewise, Paul is saying you have to renovate your mind. Go into your mind and literally pull down the thoughts, ideas, feelings, and emotions that do not belong there, which contradict the Word of God.

If you are honest, you will admit you have entertained thoughts, feelings, and emotions that you know were not in line with the Kingdom. But the question is, do you allow those things to stay and become permanent fixtures in your mind? Or, do you take authority and control over those thoughts and emotions and say, "No, you cannot reside here. You are not welcome. You do not fit. This is not the Kingdom pattern. So you do not fit. I will not let you stay!"

Now, let me ask you another question. If someone was to look at the interior design of your mind, would it match with the Word of God or would it have several mismatched items? Have you ever gone to someone's house, looked at their decor and saw it was just not matching? It didn't have a unified theme; there were no complementary or contrasting colors. Perhaps, there were some nice central things but there were also items that didn't blend with the decor.

Is your mind like that? You have holiness in there but you also have lust. You have righteousness but you also have anger. You have love but you also have a spot of rage, envy, and jealousy, which you have allowed to become permanent fixtures.

It's up to you. God did not say He is going to renovate your mind. He says you will. God speaking through Paul said, "You have to make the decision to renovate your mind. You have to rip this and that out." It is the Holy Ghost who gives you the power to rip it out. How do you rip it out?

First, confront and acknowledge that it doesn't belong there. The evil doesn't belong there; the negative feelings are out of place. That lifestyle is wrong. You make a conscious decision that these things will not be a part of your internal landscape any longer.

Let me speak from a physical, neurological perspective. Scientists say that when you hear information, you have a very short period of time to embrace that information and believe it.

Now, if that information you receive is strong enough to challenge currently held thoughts, then you literally create new pathways in your brain. That means that if you have a thought in your mind that doesn't match, you need to expose yourself to new information that is correct, Kingdom information that is correct and stronger than what you are thinking and feeling.

As you hear that information, you believe, and receive it immediately! As you believe and receive, you will literally build new inroads to your mind. That is a very practical way to begin tearing down and renovating your mind. You've got to expose yourself to information that comes up against the lies and the deceit you've been exposed to that don't belong in your mind.

When you look at the tense of the word "be transformed" (*metamorphoo* in the Greek), it suggests an ongoing process. You don't just renovate your mind one time or a couple of times; rather, you do so daily. Each day, you have to take inventory of the mind, which means paying attention to what you're thinking and feeling. You can't be indifferent to your thoughts such as *Oh, I have this thought – whatever.*

You can't just go through life not taking stock of what you're thinking or feeling. You have to be alert and pay attention. When you think, feel and want to do things that are not in line with God, you have to take authority of those things by presenting strong declarations and decrees. Use the Word of God, which is more powerful than those thoughts and feelings to override them.

Sometimes, you have to do it several times a day. It's a lifelong commitment to ensuring that your mind is in line with the Word and there's nothing that is in there that does not belong.

## Managing Your Thought Life

Here's another tool. You have to become the manager and the supervisor of your thoughts. You may not be a manager or a supervisor on your job professionally, but guess what? You have a part and a place where you could be the best manager and supervisor in the world. That is in your mind and in your heart.

Sometimes, people want to manage other people because they do not want to manage themselves. That's real talking right there. It's easy to manage everybody else to escape overseeing yourself. But at the end of the day, what you're doing is hurting you because you are allowing your mind to have thoughts and things that do not match. If your mind is not right, your conversation cannot be right. How can you ever expect to see manifestation?

> *For though we walk in the flesh, we do not war according to the flesh. For the weapons of our warfare are not carnal, but mighty through God to the pulling down of strong holds Casting down imaginations, and every high thing that exalteth itself against the knowledge of God, and bringing into captivity every thought to the obedience of Christ* (2 Corinthians 10:3 -5 KJV).

Your weapons are not physical; they are spiritual. Prayers, giving, speaking in tongues, praying in the Holy Ghost, fasting, worshiping, and praising are all spiritual weapons that do have physical ramifications or physical consequences; what you do in the spirit will have an effect on your physical experience.

But it goes further. These weapons are meant to pull down strongholds that will then build themselves in your life (See 2 Corinthians 10:4). How do strongholds build themselves in your physical life? The strongholds are like fortresses or prisons. A person is bound by something in his or her life. It didn't start on the outside first. It started in the mind. The thought was so strong, it became a physical reality. You have to cast down arguments and every high thing that exalts itself above the knowledge of God in your life.

Note that arguments and high thoughts will exalt themselves. If you are not managing your thoughts, then you're allowing arguments and things that may be against the Word of God and the Kingdom to grow and elevate themselves. As a result what started as a small seed grows into a humongous tree in your mind. It will be so big, it will bust out of your mind and manifest in your everyday life.

You may then wonder how this happened. Where did this come from? It came from small argument or thoughts that you did not check. You allowed them to remain and now, they are uncontrollable and difficult to uproot. They are not imaginary, not just in your mind, but permanent fixtures in your life. To overcome evil, you must not only cast down arguments, you also have to check your mind and ideas that are not right. Just like you check people who come up in your face, you need to check your thoughts. You had better tell your mind to line up with the Word of God. You will not play around with evil. You will not let it take root in your mind; it does not belong there.

2 Corinthians 10:4 continues by saying you have to bring every thought into captivity to the things of Christ. That is to say, every thought that comes to your mind must be examined by the rubric of God's Word to make sure it is in line with Christ. If it's not, you make it line up. Again, you have to

manage your thoughts. You cannot just live according to whatever voice you hear in your mind. Don't let your mind run your life. Govern it by the Holy Ghost. That's why He's in your life, to help you keep your mind and body in check. If you're not careful, your mind and your body will run you here and there. They will make you do things you never wanted to do. You've let your thoughts have their way for so long and let them grow so big, they are now governing you. Your body and your mind shouldn't be ruling you. Your spirit should be in charge because it can always remind you what the Word of God requires of you.

Self-talk is another tool you can use to be victorious over evil. Sometimes, you have to encourage yourself. You have to speak victory during your tests. Psalms 27 is a great passage to use when you are confronted by enemies, both natural and spiritual:

> *The Lord is my light and my salvation; whom shall I fear? the Lord is the strength of my life; of whom shall I be afraid? When the wicked, even mine enemies and my foes, came upon me to eat up my flesh, they stumbled and fell. When the wicked, even mine enemies and my foes, came upon me to eat up my flesh, they stumbled and fell. Though an host should encamp against me, my heart shall not fear: though war should rise against me, in this will I be confident. One thing have I desired of the Lord, that will I seek after; that I may dwell in the house of the Lord all the days of my life, to behold the beauty of the Lord, and to enquire in his temple* (Psalms 27:1-4).

David is talking to himself. He is building up his faith in the face of imminent and present danger, right up on him, in his face. Have you ever been up just thinking about something all the time? Were you so wrapped up in your thoughts that you had to check yourself and say, "Oh, wait a minute? I've been up in my thoughts for a long time. It started as a small thing, but it has gotten out of hand." Let's be honest; our minds and emotions can get away from us. You have to talk to yourself sometimes and say, "This is what God is. The Lord is my light, my salvation. I see danger but I declare and decree the Lord is my light and salvation. "

David could only declare that with his mouth because it was in his heart. His heart believed it. Thus, his heart declared, "I know from my experience with God that He's able to deliver me out of this. I have been attacked by this, and I've had that chasing me. I've had bears, I've had lions, I've had enemies, I've been through so many attacks. But every time Jehovah delivered me. He had a promise on my life. I was anointed for a purpose and I couldn't go anywhere until that purpose was fulfilled. So, I'm not going to be shaken by this present danger, for I know that the LORD is a very present help in the time of trouble. " Just as David had to speak to himself, sometimes you have to talk to yourself to get your mind right.

Talk to yourself and tell yourself what you are going to do:

- I will believe God.
- I will trust God.
- It's going to get better.
- I know my mind is all over the place, but my mind is lined up with the Word.

- My mind is stable.
- My mind is at peace.
- My heart is set.
- My heart is fixed on God.
- I am not divided.
- I am not double-minded.
- I am single-minded.
- My mind is made up.
- My answer is "Yes, Lord."
- My ways are God's ways.
- My will is submitted to God's word.

Sometimes, you just have to tell your mind, *Be quiet. Heart, you need to get it all together*. Just like you tell people to hush and get out of your face, you must command your mind to be quiet, hear the Word of the Lord, believe the Word of the Lord, and be governed by the Word of God.

**Three Worldly Gateways**

Connected to self-talk is taking control over your gates – your five senses. Be careful what you see, watch, listen to, consume physically and mentally, who you are around, who you touch, and who you come into contact with physically. You know covenant; that's why even who you have sex with also influences your inner being. And if you are not having sex, you still have to be careful with whom you are having intimate covenant conversations; all these things impact your inner self.

There are three worldly gateways you want to stay away from. *"For all that is in the world, the lust of the flesh, and the lust of the eyes, and the pride of life, is not of the Father, but is of the world"* (John 2:16). The lust of the flesh is number one; the lust of the eyes is number two, and the pride of life is number three.

The lust of the flesh is physical pleasure. You have to make sure you are not governed by the desire to please your flesh. If it doesn't feel good, you don't like it. Now, let's be honest: everything in God is not going to feel good to your flesh. Sometimes, you have to be selfless for the cause of Christ. For instance, when you are fasting and turn down your plate, your body is not going to like that especially if you like to eat. Your body doesn't want to suffer. That's why a lot of people don't work out because their bodies are crying. Your body doesn't want to go through the stress you're putting it through when you're running or lifting weights: it's called restraint. You only want what feels good. Not just in terms of not putting the body under unnecessary stress but craving things that make us feel good even though, ultimately, they are bad for us. Why is it most of the food that tastes delicious is not good for you? You love it because it makes you feel good. That's why there is comfort food. Know this, no comfort food is healthy. You cannot crave physical pleasure over pleasing God. If you want something in your flesh that will cause you not to please God and to not represent Him well, then you have to check that thing because lust will lead you to sin and sin will lead you to death (See James 1:15).

The second worldly gate is the lust of the eyes or craving for everything you see. It's part of human nature to want everything you like when you see it. Have you ever taken a child into a store and everything she saw, she wanted? First, she wanted the Barbie doll. Then, she wanted the dollhouse. Next, she wanted candy. She wanted the bubble gum. Before that she wanted chips but this time, it's the pickles. This example is about children, but how many adults are like that?

You crave fame, importance, status, material possessions, money and all the things you see. You watch other people and begin to envy and long for what they have. You would do almost anything to get it. There's a generation of believers who are willing to do anything, even ungodly, immoral things just to have the things their eyes cause them to lust for.

The third worldly gate is the pride of life or being proud of your achievements and possessions. Some people are haughty, arrogant, and cocky because they are, in some way, convinced that everything they have acquired and done is because of them. Anyone who has any good sense knows, if it was not for the Lord, they would have nothing and would have achieved nothing.

It is the Lord working in you that has given you this success. But you cannot become prideful and conceited. Some believers have been hindered from seeing manifestations because God knows they will become proud. Imagine, God has blessed you, but you act as if you did it yourself. You neither give God the glory nor do you use your possessions and opportunities to glorify God. A good way to measure if you will become proud with an increase is to look at how prideful you are with what you have now. If you're prideful with what you have now, what makes you think that you're not going to be even more prideful if God gave you more?

Another tool for developing a mindset that leads to manifestation is making sure that you do not have an ungodly love for money. The Bible is clear that the love of money is the root of all evil (See 1 Timothy 6:10). Yes, money is a defense and God wants us to be healthy and prosper. He wants us to have material possessions. That's all very true but at the same time, some people lust for money. *Eros* is the word that means sexual, erotic love but some people lust after money like they lust after a person; they have to get it at any cost. These people are willing to sacrifice their morals, values, principles, faith, religion, family, friends, and even themselves just to get more. It doesn't matter how much they have; it's never enough.

So, I urge you to be intentional and strategic in your thought life. You cannot be haphazard. If you do not manage your thought life, it will manage you. How can you strategically manage your thought life? You have to intentionally meditate on specific things.

**Making Philippians 4:6-8 Your Lifestyle**

*"Be careful for nothing; but in everything by prayer and supplication with thanksgiving let your requests be made known unto God"* (Philippians 4:6 KJV).

Here is a great biblical solution for anxiety. A lot of people have anxiety attacks and a lot of believers suffer from panic. To prevent yourself from becoming anxious and having panic attacks, you must constantly pray and earnestly make your request to God, while thanking Him. Many times, we become anxious or panic-stricken because we are overwhelmed by those thoughts of how we will do one thing or the other, how we will pay for this or how we will overcome that? You become so overwhelmed and consumed with your thoughts that you panic. You should replace your anxiety with prayers, supplications, and thanksgiving.

Talk to God: *Lord, I can't hold this in here because if I hold it in my head, it will wear me out. I'm overwhelmed; I'm stressed; I'm sweating; I'm frustrated; I'm just all over the place.* Tell God. Make it known. *God, this is the situation. God this is what I need. I trust You for it. I believe for it and I'm going to thank You in advance."* Nothing seals and accelerates your requests like thanksgiving. If you can thank God before you have something, it is an indication of your faith that God has heard you. God is able, and God is going to meet your needs. That is a solution to anxiety. That is a freebie right there.

*"And the peace of God, which passeth all understanding, shall keep your hearts and minds through Christ Jesus"* (Philippians 4:7 KJV).

Keep your heart with all vigilance because out of it flows the wellsprings of life. How do you guard and keep your mind and heart? By constantly making your requests known to God, with thanksgiving. In doing so, you will reduce anxiety, bring peace to your mind, and guard it from attack.

Finally, this verse says to meditate on these things: whatsoever is true, noble or honorable, just, pure, lovely, of a good report, (not gossip, not the negative), virtuous and praiseworthy, meditate on these things (See Philippians 4:8). To meditate, literally means to repeat the same thing over and over again under your breath. It's not what other religions call meditation, which is connected to breathing and listening to a mantra or beats. That's not Biblical meditation. What I'm talking about is the repetition of the words that are true. You know God is faithful; you know His Word is true. He doesn't lie. He's faithful to His Word. These are things that you know are true. You have to think about these things and constantly repeat them in your mind so they become a part of your landscape. If you practice meditation, you will literally furnish your mind with good virtues. If you don't do so, and constantly think about fears, offenses or lustful thoughts, you give way to worldly, evil thoughts that will consume your mind. You have to be intentional about what you furnish your mind with.

If your mind is protected, it becomes good and holy. Then, your conversations will reflect that. In many ways, you will see your life lining up with your words because your words are lined up with your mind and your mind is lined up with the Word of God.

During Job's afflictions, God invited him into a countercultural experience, and showed him how the Kingdom operates. God gave Job a Kingdom experience in the middle of his tragedy. Make commanding your morning a countercultural experience. It's a Kingdom invitation that will significantly transform your life.

# CHAPTER 4

THE MOUTH:
THE GATEWAY TO REALITY

In the previous chapters we defined "to declare" as to speak and make statements in a bold and serious fashion. "To decree" is a legal term to mean speaking from the authority of someone who has the ability to give that authority, and we know that relationship with Jesus gives us that authority. So, when you decree a thing, be very clear that Heaven is backing up your statements. And when you get up first thing in the morning, determine to take your rightful place as a son of God and make statements about how your day is going to be.

Because guess what? Whether you make declarations or not, the day has already made plans for you, so you might as well go ahead and determine what that day is going to be. Everything that the day has planned that is not in concert with the will of God, we command that thing to die and fall. We declare a course that is in the will of God and, as the Holy Spirit prays through us and as we pray the will of God, we expect to see those things to happen in our life. Now, they may not happen all at once, but the more we proclaim them every day by faith and praying in the spirit, the stronger it gets, and the more we begin to see those declarations manifest.

God has given me three Ms that are essential to commanding your morning: your mind, your mouth and your manifestation. This chapter is designed to share information with you about the second M – the mouth, which is the gateway to reality.

**Your Heart**

So, I want to start with this understanding about the mouth. The origin of your words does not start in your mouth but in your heart. That's a very important principle. And when I say origin, we're talking about the source from where it all comes. Your mouth may be the channel from which words are released but those words start in your heart.

Proverbs 4:23-24 says:

*Keep your heart with all diligence,
For out of it spring the issues of life.
Put away from you a deceitful mouth,
And put perverse lips far from you.*

The word "keep" in this context suggests that you have to fight to protect your heart. You have to be a watchman over it. If there's anything that you need to guard in yourself, it should be primarily your heart.

Why? The heart is the internal part of you. Here, we are talking about the core, the center of you, where your emotions, your intellect and your will are housed. So, you have to guard, look over, protect, watch, defend that internal part of you as the most important thing inside of you. That is the base from which everything pertaining to your life comes from. Everything that your life will ever see flows from there.

**Your Mouth**

But then the above scripture goes on to urge you to put away from you a deceitful mouth. Verse 23 says from out of your heart flow the springs of life and then it suddenly jumps to "a deceitful mouth." How did it go from heart to mouth? Where does this spring come from and where does it go? It springs out of the heart and flows out from the heart through the mouth. So, the mouth is the exit of the heart; this is so important. And so, the way that we know what is in the person's heart is what's coming out of their mouth.

Out of your mouth come words that become the paint brush that begins to shape your day. Your tone becomes the color palette dipped into by the paint brush and your life becomes the canvas upon which your day – and life – are splashed with color.

**Your Stomach**

Now I want to share some very important scriptures to lay a foundation for your words and their manifestation. One of the key scriptures that we want to tap into is this:

> *A man's stomach will be satisfied with the fruit of his mouth; He will be satisfied with the consequence of his words. Death and life are in the power of the tongue, And those who love it and indulge it will eat its fruit and bear the consequences of their words.* (Proverbs 19:20-21 AMP).

What a powerful revelation! Here, the stomach refers to the internal parts of the man which are separate from the heart. If the heart houses the emotions, the will and the intellect, the stomach talks about the complete internal aspect of the person. If you were to think about where the Holy Spirit dwells in you, it would really be in your stomach or belly.

Of course, the stomach is not literally where the Holy Spirit dwells, for He cannot just be contained in one place. But when your mind connects to the idea of being filled, it is linked to the stomach. Your stomach or your internal life is that which sustains you. The stomach is the place where food is digested and broken down to carry nutrients to the entire body and supply it with energy. And one of the ways that energy or driving-force is expressed is by what comes out of your mouth. If fruit here means the evidence of the outcome, whatever your life is experiencing is a direct result of the fruit of your mouth.

## The Power of the Tongue

How does your mouth produce fruit? Through the words that you release. In turn, those very same words you release will cause you to be filled. Now, here is what you're going to be filled with: death or life. Either your fruit is going to be dead produce or your fruit is going to be living produce depending upon the kind of words that come out of your mouth.

You may say, "Well, sometimes I have bad days and I get mad, and say things where my emotions get the better of me. But that's okay, God understands, right? The things I may say then may not really be a true indicator of my heart." Yes, we all have bad days where we tend to be off-guard. I'm not talking about these occasional slips and bad days; I'm talking about a continuous build up. If you are continuously speaking death, speaking negativity, speaking lies and twisting things, if that is the greater part of your conversation, then you're feeding your life with negativity – and that brings death. Your negative words are dispensing death all around, even to yourself.

That's so powerful: the idea that you and I become partakers of our own words. That means you don't get to just put words out there and leave them hanging in the air, the Bible says that you will be the first to partake of them. Verse 21, says *"Death and life are in the power of the tongue."* Note the order of importance – "death and life" not "life and death" – which tells me that you can kill a thing faster than you can bring it to a life with your words.

When I began to really meditate on this and see what God was showing me, it was an "Aha" moment for me. I don't think we realize how powerful our words are. How many people are releasing death not only over the people that they're speaking bad about, but over their own life?

But today, I choose to speak life. I choose to declare blessings. I choose to speak about that which is good, that which is noble, that which is pure, that which is honest, that which is of good report. My mind will constantly rehearse psalms, hymns and spiritual songs. Because, as I speak life and I speak blessings and positivity, I am producing fruit for others. And that same blessing, that same positivity, that same truth that I'm speaking out to others in every situation becomes my portion, too.

Let me ask you then, what kind of diet are you feeding yourself with? Most of us wish to eat right and so what's on your plate is going to be what's good for you, mostly healthy nutrients. But if you load your plate with empty calories and harmful substances such as fries and sugary things, carbs and starches, then you are putting death into your body. And the body begins to respond to what you feed it. Similarly, you know what kind of diet you are producing for your soul by paying attention to what forms the bulk of your words.

And, listen, it says it's *"in the power of the tongue."* That word "power" has the same meaning as "in your hands." In other words, you have death and life in your hands. You have power over whether you're going to produce a diet of death or a diet of life for yourself. How do you have power? By exercising control over your tongue and what comes out of your mouth.

We have to work hard to get control over our tongues because it is a fire that can set the forest of your entire life ablaze. James 3:5-10 tells us:

> *Even so the tongue is a little member and boasts great things. See how great a forest a little fire kindles! And the tongue is a fire, a world*

*of iniquity. The tongue is so set among our members that it defiles the whole body, and sets on fire the course of nature; and it is set on fire by hell. For every kind of beast and bird, of reptile and creature of the sea, is tamed and has been tamed by mankind. But no man can tame the tongue. It is an unruly evil, full of deadly poison. With it we bless our God and Father, and with it we curse men, who have been made in the similitude of God. Out of the same mouth proceed blessing and cursing. My brethren, these things ought not to be so.*

When we have a double-forked tongue speaking blessings and curses, it produces a perverseness in our lives. Perverse means against the standard or to intentionally behave in a way that is unreasonable, despite the consequences. The Bible gives us warnings about this type of action. Proverbs 15:4 states, *"A wholesome tongue is a tree of life: but perverseness therein is a breach in the spirit."* When we have a perverse tongue (purposely speaking against the standard and will of God), we create an opening in our spirit which gives way to an attack from the enemy. You must know that you are hedged in and protected by God just like Job. But it was his words about what he feared that created a breach:

*What I feared has come upon me; what I dreaded has happened to me* (Job 3:25).

Here is another fascinating scripture about how the enemy attacks those who breach hedges:

*He who digs a pit will fall into it, And whoever breaks through a wall will be bitten by a serpent* (Ecclesiastes 10:8).

Guard your tongue Commander and prevent unnecessary assaults from the devil.

**Power to Create**

So, then your tongue becomes the divine pen of creation in your reality. Now, let me tell you why this is so important. We are made in God's image and likeness because we have His spirit in us. Therefore, we have the ability to create just as He created. How did Elohim create? Elohim created by speaking, that is, releasing words into the atmosphere. The only thing that Elohim did not create by speaking was Adam. For Adam, He breathed the breath of life into him, breathing His own likeness into him (Genesis 1:26) so that man, too, could also experience the ability to create.

Think about it. God says, "I'm going to form you with my hand and endue you with the power to create because My Spirit resides within you." So, since you have the Holy Spirit living on the inside of you, you have the ability to create with your words. You can create death or you can create life, and whatever you choose to create is the fruit that you're going to consume in your life.

I want to point out the following to you because I think it's very important. The framers of the Hebrew language understood the power of God's word when they decided to use the same Hebrew term *dabar* to express the concept of "word" and "thing." This was because the word coming out of God's mouth was so potent that the moment He said it, it came into existence as a thing. When you release words into the air, they also come into existence even though you haven't yet seen the manifestation. But believe that if you release words, they become things in the spirit realm waiting to manifest in the physical realm.

So, I pray that you have blessings ready to manifest, you have increase ready to manifest, and you have love ready to manifest in your life. I pray that you don't have negative things, lies and curses ready to manifest because whatever you're releasing out of your mouth is what you are putting out there in the atmosphere to produce fruit at some point in your life.

As covenant people, we get to make the choice every day of what words we will speak. Your words become the gateway to your reality. So, my question is, what kind of reality do you want to see? Are all your words commensurate with the reality you want to see?

Let's get deeper. Jesus tells us, "... *by your words you will be justified, and by your words you will be condemned*" (Matthew 12:37). This means your words are so powerful that they can vindicate or condemn you. Jesus says we have a choice:

> *Either make the tree good and its fruit good, or else make the tree bad and its fruit bad; for a tree is known by its fruit* (Matthew 12:33).

You've got to produce what you say you are because the only evidence the outside world has that you are who you say you are is the fruit you produce. Some people maintain they are good people but, if your words are evil, then you are evil. You say you love God but, if the words you use do not demonstrate a true sold-out commitment in your heart to God, then what is the reality?

**Out of the Abundance**

Jesus, looking at the religious leaders of His day, saw beyond their ceremonial and religious garb. He saw right into their hearts and knew that their hearts did not match their outward robes of righteousness. He called them out for what they really were:

> *Brood of vipers! How can you, being evil, speak good things? For out of the abundance of the heart the mouth speaks. A good man out of the good treasure of his heart brings forth good things, and an evil man out of the evil treasure brings forth evil things* (Matthew 12:34-35).

*"For out of the abundance of the heart, the mouth speaks."* Out of the overflow of the heart, the issues of life spring forth. They come from the heart and are released through the mouth.

My friend, pay attention to the words that come out of people's mouths to discern what spirit they are. You can't convince me that people are somehow different from how they consistently talk. The operative word is consistent. What does most of their conversation consist of? If it's lies and gossip, you can't trust anything that person says. If you continue in a covenant relationship with a person like this, then don't be surprised if your life is full of drama, disorder, and confusion. But, if you are a person that's passionate for Kingdom business and advancing God's purpose, you don't have time to be connected with a person who is negative, evil, deceitful, jealous and hateful in conversation.

**The Danger of Idle Talk**

Come on saints, we've got to stop living in deception and naïveté. We must pay attention to our words as well as other people's words: either we are good or producing evil, positive or negative, life-producing or death-producing. When people show you who they are, you'd better believe them. How do they show you? By their words and their actions, however well they try to convince you to the contrary.

Therefore, take heed of Jesus' warning: *"But I say to you that for every idle word men may speak, they will give account of it in the day of judgment"* (Matthew 12:36). *"Idle"* means there's loose talk, speaking without thinking, speaking without concern for the effects of your words or the impact that your words have, because every word we release out of our mouth, we are going to have to explain it to God.

*"For by your words you will be justified, and by your words you will be condemned."* This is awesome! Our words will impact our eternity. Our righteousness or our guilt is determined and judged by God based on our words.

You might say, "You mean to tell me that you can tell a person has been justified or the person is bound for hell from their words?"

"Yes, that's what I'm telling you."

You might say, "That's a lot. I don't believe that. I thought it's the condition of your heart. It's about who you really are. I've got a good heart."

"But if you have a good heart, then your mouth is going to speak good is what the Bible is saying."

Yes, you have a good heart but you never have anything good to say about anybody. The truth is your heart is not good; you are deceived and you're trying to deceive other people around you. You cannot say you have a good heart and your mouth is evil. The two things are not compatible. And you're speaking condemnation on yourself when you continue to speak death and negativity. But when you choose to speak life, not only are you releasing produce that will feed your life and cause you to grow but you're also walking and living in the righteousness that has been imputed to us by faith in Jesus Christ.

I cannot stress enough the weight of our words because they have a direct consequence on our eternity. Our words are a sure indicator of whether our heart is really converted. So, people can say they are saved all day long. "Oh, yes. I love the Lord. I believe in God. I go to church" – all that is great. But what is your mouth saying mostly? If your mouth is not talking like a person that's been redeemed and washed in the blood of Jesus, I don't care what you're saying. Your heart is not lining up with your words. But if the greater part of your conversation is life-giving and blessing and speaking forth God's marvellous works, that shows you are of a different spirit.

**Blessings and Curses**

Just as you could be justified or condemned by your words, you can also bless or curse with your words. Look at Deuteronomy 11:

> *Behold, I set before you today a blessing and a curse: the blessing, if you obey the commandments of the Lord your God which I command you today; and the curse, if you do not obey the commandments of the Lord your God, but turn aside from the way which I command you today, to go after other gods which you have not known* (Deuteronomy 11:26-28).

In this situation, Jehovah is making an agreement with Israel. He's laid down certain guidelines or commandments, rules, laws they are to follow. If they obey those commandments, then they are going to walk in blessing but if they choose to disobey, they would be walking in curses.

Blessings and curses are evoked primarily by words. To bless (*barak* in Hebrew, *eulogei* in Greek), means to speak well of, to speak highly of, to commend. So, you can speak well of yourself, bless yourself, your family, your friends, your church, your organization, your community, your nation; you can bless the world. The Bible even says to bless your enemies, and pray for those who despitefully use you.

However, if we choose to do the opposite and curse ourselves or others, we will inherit the curse instead. Let's make sure that we are not walking around speaking ill of people, wishing and declaring bad things over them. Ask yourself how much of your life right now is being affected by a blessing or a curse that somebody spoke over you and you believed? That's the key. For a word of blessing or a word of curse to take root, you have to receive either the blessing or the curse. When someone says, "I bless you in the name of the Lord. I declare that God will prosper you this day," you'll say, "Amen, I receive it," meaning "It is so. I agree with it."

I know a lady, whose son I was mentoring, and she would randomly disrespect him: "I can't stand you! You're nothing! You're dumb! You're going to be this and that!" When I admonished her and asked her why she was doing that, she replied, "Well, he reminds me of his daddy and I hate his daddy!"

"So, because of your hatred for his daddy, you're taking it out on him and you're speaking negatively over his life before it can even get started?" I said.

But if she is going to tell me she's a good church-going person who loves the Lord, how can that be? It's not possible.

Hear me saints. Maybe you're saying, I'm being really harsh with this person. No. I'm not being self-righteous and I'm not being judgmental. I'm just saying we have to know where to draw the line. You cannot tell me that you are a good person when you are constantly speaking negatively over your child because of something outside of his control. The fact that you hate his daddy is another indication that something is not right with your heart. Get it right. Unforgiveness will block manifestation, blessings, and favor in your life!

But some rush to defend her, "Oh, she's a good person. Don't judge her. She's just been through some challenges and can't help herself." Saints, why are we defending this foolishness? Stop it now. Stop participating in death. You are enabling curses over someone before they can even have a head start on life by excusing those words. But thanks be to God! If He has blessed you, then no one can curse you.

**The Blessing Stands**

The prophet Balaam was hired by Balak, King of Moab to curse Israel. But Israel had already been blessed by God and so every time Balaam would go out to try curse Israel, he would turn around and start blessing them. He couldn't curse what God had blessed:

> *If Balak were to give me his house full of silver and gold, I could not go beyond the word of the Lord, to do good or bad of my own will. What the Lord says, that I must speak* (Numbers 24:13).

Ironically, in Numbers 25 we clearly see how the Israelites cursed themselves and that was to commit acts of harlotry with the Moabite women. In doing so, they violated the Deuteronomy 11 covenant you read previously. You see, when you're in alignment with the covenant or the commandment or the agreement, you're under the safety of the blessing. But when you violate the terms and the conditions, you have no protection; the blessings cannot protect you from the curse.

The essence of the blessing is to know your identity in Christ. You have to know that you have already been blessed. And, if you have already been blessed, nobody can curse you. The only way that a curse can be activated in the life of a blessed person is that they believe the lie of the curse. Or that they break covenant and position them in a place where they bring curses upon themselves.

To bring this chapter to a close, you and I have to intentionally manage our tongue and be mindful of our conversation. We can't just indulge in idle speech and then say, "Oh, I didn't mean it," or "I'm just talking," or "I'm just running my mouth." The spirit world does not know that you are just playing. It hears words and then creates things that will manifest in due time. We can't expect to let our tongue just have its way and then expect positive or productive things to manifest in our life. We need to be very specific, strategic and intentional with the words that we are using if we expect to make our way successful.

**Scriptures to Declare**

I'm going to be very frank with you. If you know that managing your tongue is a challenge for you, then I encourage you to seek professional help. Also, I want to encourage you to begin to declare the following scriptures over your life every day. You don't have to declare all of them at once but take a couple of them a day, and once that's declared over your life, you have to do your part to bring your tongue into subjection.

> *He who would love life And see good days, Let him refrain his tongue from evil, And his lips from speaking deceit* (1 Peter 3:10).

Now, this is how you would declare it: "Because I love life and want to see good days, I refrain my tongue from evil and my lips from speaking deceit."

> *Whoever guards his mouth and tongue keeps his soul from troubles* (Proverbs 21:23).

So, if your soul is in trouble, then you need to guard your mouth and tongue. You need to say, "Because I guard my mouth and tongue, I declare that my soul is out of trouble." Glory!

> *Keep your tongue from evil, And your lips from speaking deceit* (Songs 34:13).

Confess: "I keep my tongue from evil, and my lips from speaking deceit."

> *Set a guard, O Lord, over my mouth; Keep watch over the door of my lips* (Songs 141:3).

This is for the one that says, "I can't do this on my own. I need help from the Lord." You can just declare that straight up. "Set a guard, O Lord, over my mouth and keep watch over the door of my lips because I don't even trust myself to control what's coming out of my mouth. Hey, it's alright to be honest. You can't get healed and delivered unless you're honest.

> *There is one who speaks like the piercings of a sword, But the tongue of the wise promotes health. The truthful lip shall be established*

*forever, But a lying tongue is but for a moment* (Proverbs 12:18-19).

Some of us are very skilled at using our tongue to cut people. Our tongue is like a sword always speaking sharply at people; that is no different from having an evil tongue. So, you may not curse people outright and you may not say bad things. But if you have a sharp tongue and are quick with your words – some call it being witty – I say, watch yourself! That's not a wise tongue. It doesn't produce life or promote health.

So, you need to say, "Lord, I declare and decree that my tongue is no longer like the piercings of a sword. But I declare and decree that I have the tongue of the wise. And, because I have the tongue of the wise, I produce health. And I declare and decree that, because I have a truthful tongue, I shall be established forever."

*He who has knowledge spares his words, And a man of understanding is of a calm spirit. Even a fool is counted wise when he holds his peace; When he shuts his lips, he is considered perceptive* (Proverbs 17:27-28).

Now this scripture really hit me hard. You can't tell me that you are a person of wisdom and knowledge and your spirit is like a raging bull all of the time. Because the Bible says that a man of understanding has a calm even-keeled spirit. And this is how powerful a calm, even-keeled demeanor is: even when you have a fool that acts calm, people will think that person is wise.

How can a fool appear to be wise? When he has enough sense not to continue in an argument that is becoming contentious. Many people who claim to be wise cannot stop themselves and shut their mouth. As a result, they get into unnecessary conflict. Let's learn from the fool.

So, say with me: "Because I have knowledge I do not speak loosely. Because I have understanding I have a calm spirit."

# CHAPTER 5

THE MECHANICS OF MANIFESTATION

The Mechanics of Manifestation is the final aspect of manifestation. Mechanics is the machinery or the working parts of something but it also suggests the dynamics of movement. If you were to open up your watch, inside you would see the mechanics, the different pieces, apparatus, and systems that make your watch work.

We have already defined manifestation as the tangible expression of an abstract idea, concept, or principle. Manifestation is marked by an event, an action, or an object as proof that this thing has transitioned from the invisible to the visible. You cannot say you have a manifestation, if you cannot pinpoint that action, event or an object to indicate that the transition has happened. Learning the mechanics of manifestation is important because when you know the internal workings, then you can replicate it again and at will. Getting consistent results in prayer hinges on knowing how and why you got results!

How do we move our thoughts to words and then to manifestations? There are at least six steps in the mechanics of manifestation.

**Step Number One: Guard Your Heart**

We have established in Chapter 4 that your thought produces words and your words emanate from your heart. *"Keep thy heart with all diligence; for out of it are the issues of life. Put away from thee a froward mouth, and perverse lips put far from thee"* (Proverbs 4:23-24).

The mouth is the gateway to your reality. Then out of your heart, that houses your emotions, your will and your intellect, flow the words. The progression is from thoughts to words and from words to things. The mechanics is based on the creative power of words because Elohim the Creator God can take nothing and make something by just speaking it into existence. Because we are made in the image and likeness of Elohim, He has given us the ability to speak a thing and it manifests. You, who were made in the image of God, when you speak by faith and accordance to the will and word of God, your words also become things.

I say that to emphasize that your thought life and your words must be influenced by purpose. Therefore, you think and you speak things that are in line with your divine purpose. Why are you alive? Why are you in the earth? Why are you in this specific place or circumstance? You're here for a reason, so your words and your thoughts must be influenced by your purpose.

You're not just speaking random words. You are speaking things that will cause the Kingdom agenda to be advanced and sustained. Your purpose is to find your place in that agenda and to think and speak the thing that's going to advance that purpose. If they are not in line with your purpose and if they are not advancing the Kingdom agenda, you should not entertain those thoughts and those thoughts should not become words. Otherwise, you're producing things that run contradictory to the Kingdom.

**Step Number Two: Exercise Your faith**

The second step is to believe that your words have been released in the spirit realm and will accomplish their purpose. Although they are still invisible, they have not vanished into thin air. You cannot see them but they exist. You must by faith understand that the worlds were framed by the word of God, so that the things which are seen were not made of things which are visible (See Hebrews 11:3). The words that you speak are contained and stored in the spirit realm, in the invisible.

You must understand that when you declare a word, it is established by God in the spirit realm. It remains invisible to you until the time of its manifestation. That word is already a *dabar* that came out of your mouth and has become a *dabar* thing that already has an existence in the spirit.

Believing in this principle requires faith. We want to have the faith that the moment we declare and decree a thing, we can believe it has already come into existence. That is the confidence that you must walk in.

The problem with so many Christians is we are waiting to see it before we believe it. But the Bible says we've got to believe the moment we speak it. It's a done deal. The biggest challenge then is transitioning from the physical eyes to the eyes of faith. That's why Hebrews 11:1 tells you *"Now faith is the substance of things hoped for."* Faith is the evidence of what we are expecting but have not yet seen. One translation says that faith is the title deed, the deed of ownership of a possession. It is the thing that you hold on to until it has manifested itself in the physical realm.

2 Corinthians 5:7 says we walk by faith not by sight. That word "walk" (*peripateo* in the Greek) figuratively, means to live, deport oneself, and follow. This suggests a pattern of walking. It's talking about your lifestyle. You live by faith, not by what you see. The problem is so many people are living by what they can see versus living by what they believe.

Believe that faith is real in the spirit realm and when you open your mouth by faith and declare a thing that Heaven is endorsing it and backing it up. Although you cannot see the process, believe that it is there and know that at the appointed time it will come into manifestation. Walk with confidence in that reality. Believe that it's already yours before you see it.

You see, if you don't believe that it's yours before you see it, then you don't have it and you won't get it until you believe. What's delaying some people right now is that you don't believe it's there just because you spoke it. You're looking for physical evidence. The evidence will not be there if you don't believe that you spoke it into existence.

Believe that the thing you spoke is in the spirit realm, hovering over your life or the assigned place, waiting to manifest in your life. If you spoke a word over your children, when you speak the word, it leaves your mouth and it goes in the spirit realm and is hovering over your children's life until the appointed time for manifestation. If you spoke over your job, if you spoke over your finances, just know when that *dabar* or logos came out in your mouth, it is travelling in the spirit realm, and it is hovering over that thing, that place, that circumstance until the appointed time for manifestation.

Look up right now and say, *"Every word that I've spoken over my life is hovering over me right now. I may not see it yet but I know it is there. It's over my life. It's following my life."* I command it to come inside and manifest in my life. That word over my life is what's protecting me because, when I spoke that word, God backed it up, and He will deliver according to His promises.

If those words don't come to pass, then God's name fails, but God will never fail. The whole existence of the universe rests upon God being true to His Word. Here is His assurance:

> *For my thoughts are not your thoughts, neither are your ways my ways, saith the Lord. For as the heavens are higher than the earth, so are my ways higher than your ways, and my thoughts than your*

*thoughts. For as the rain cometh down, and the snow from heaven, and returneth not thither, but watereth the earth, and maketh it bring forth and bud, that it may give seed to the sower, and bread to the eater: So shall my **word** be that goeth forth out of my mouth: it shall not return unto me void, but it shall accomplish that which I please, and it shall prosper in the thing whereto I sent it* (Isaiah 55:8-11 KJV, emphasis added).

Now, that the term for word in verse 11 is *dabar*, in other words, "So shall my *dabar* be that goes forth out of My mouth." Notice that the *dabar* is going out of God's mouth. That is the release of the word and it does not come back to God void. It won't be ineffective. It's going to get the results. It's going to accomplish His purpose.

You got to believe that when you open your mouth and speak a word, God is taking that word in the spirit and He's making it, He's forming it because, remember, God has everything. He is self-existing. He has everything inside of Himself to be and whatever He needs to make and create is already contained in Him.

God's word is now birthed; it will prosper in the thing it was sent to do. The word *prosper* (*ve·hitz·li·ach* in the Hebrew) means to advance or succeed. That means there's nothing that can block this word when the time comes for it to manifest. It's not going to get lost trying to find your son or daughter or financial breakthrough. The word is sure in its direction and it will find the place where you sent it. When it gets there, it will hover over that place or person until it's time for its entry. What determines the entry? It is the timing of the Lord. Wrap your heart and mind around that.

### Step Number Three: Expect a Fight

While you are in limbo waiting for manifestation, there may be warfare to delay it from coming to pass. Be sensitive to the fact that there may be opposition from the enemy. The enemy does not want your word to come to pass. He cannot stop the manifestation but he can delay the manifestation and your position of faith.

The delay may cause you to speak words that kill your own manifestation. See, the enemy can't kill it but he can make you kill it. He cannot kill anything you've spoken but he can frustrate you and make you think and speak religiously – "If it is God's will …" until you turn around and cancel your faith-filled words.

How do you sense that the manifestation of your words is under attack? There are three signs.

**An Unusual Delay.** You've got to get to a place of confidence by faith that, when you speak a word, you should expect very rapid manifestation.

I believe that we are in the season of Amos 9:13 where the plowman will *overtake* the *reaper* and the treader of grapes, *the sower* of seed, meaning an acceleration in the coming of things. In fact, when you think it, God is partnering with your thoughts. Before you will speak it, He's already doing it. By the time you speak it, it's already done.

Why are you sitting around thinking that it takes ten years for God to manifest what you're saying? That is religiosity when you keep saying, "Oh, but I'm just going to wait on the Lord." Listen, by all means wait on Him, but when you use that scripture it's really talking about serving. You are active while you wait. You're not sitting around with your arms folded. You are busy working, waiting for God to refresh your spirit to move on to the next stage.

Here is another thing. When you have an active prayer life and spiritual life with God, you may begin to feel something in your spirit in not right like Daniel when he prayed for the return of the captives from Babylon (See Daniel 10).

When Daniel set his heart to understand what was really going on, he understood that fasting would move the hand of God. Some of you all, if you're experiencing unusual delays or you feel like your word and manifestation is under attack, fast. Get into spirit. Turn down the things that are not pleasant.

Daniel's fast lasted 21 days but the principle was that he was going to fast as long as it took until he got answers.

Fasting brings answers. If you're fasting right, you going to focus on God and, when you deny your flesh to the pleasant things, it opens up your spirit and help you to see into the spirit clearly.

Just as demonic principalities in the spirit realm were delaying Daniel's answer, so too will some of your delays come from demonic spirits that do not want your breakthrough. But you need to tell those spirits, "Loose your hold on my manifestation. You're not going to keep me down so that you can benefit from me being down. I'm going to progress. I'm going to increase and I'm going to move into what God has for me."

**The Spirit of Pisgah.** You could be at the edge of the promise and then you seem to encounter an obstruction. Remember Deuteronomy 34: 1-4 where the Lord takes Moses up to mount Nebo to Pisgah, which means pinnacle or height, and shows him all the dimensions of the Promised Land and He says, "I'm letting you see what I swear to your father Abraham, Isaac, and Jacob but you won't go over. You will not cross over." The spirit of Pisgah is that same spirit that gets you to the edge of your promise but it hinders you from crossing over to possess what God has promised.

You spoke the job. You declared the increase. You declared the salary raise. You declared a turnaround for the husband. You declared salvation for the household. You declared healing over someone. Now, you're at the edge. You can see it. You know it's your season. You can see it but you seem to be hindered.

Here's the religious spirit that causes you to kill that word when you say, "*I guess it's just not my time. I guess it's just not God's will for me yet. I guess it's just isn't my time to have this job. I guess it's just isn't my time to be healed. I guess it's just isn't my time to get whatever.*" You released a word and then cancel it out by what you speak.

Refuse to let Pisgah stop you from crossing over by convincing you to be religious and say it wasn't your time. The devil is a liar. Speak, claim, and fight for what God says is yours.

**The Desire to Faint.** Have you ever found yourself in a place where you were about to faint, give up, find all hell broke loose? Everything that could go wrong goes wrong. And you're just at the point where you think, *I'm just tired of waiting for this thing to manifest. I'm just tired of believing and hoping and I just might as well give up.*

When you feel so pressured in that you're about to give up on what God promised, that is a sign that you are at the edge of a due season. You're getting ready to experience the manifestation. "*And let us not grow weary while doing good, for in due season we shall reap if we do not lose heart"* (Galatians 6:9). Fainting causes you to forfeit the manifestation.

Remember, the enemy cannot stop the manifestation but he can cause you to forfeit your manifestation by giving up. When you speak failure, in the spirit realm it bumps into what you've already declared and it destroys it because the frustration and the anger is stronger than your word of faith.

But let me tell you something about faith. You are in a fixed fight. Everything that God says is yours that you have declared is yours. So, declare and decree today that you will not faint, you will not give up, you will not retreat from what God says is yours. Declare and decree in the name of Jesus that you are standing your ground by faith.

You will possess. You will crossover. You will wade in that water. You are going to cross your Jordan. You're coming out on the other side safely. You will move into the Canaan that God has for you and you will not allow the devil to set you up, to speak, to cancel, to nullify, and to void what you said. God's word cannot return void; neither can yours. Rebuke the spirit to cancel your own words in the name of the Lord Jesus.

**Step Number Four: Visualize Your Manifestation**

While you are in the in-between phase, in limbo, you must also see that thing as if it's already manifested in your life before you have it. Step four is visualization and it is based on the law of attraction. This is not a secular principle. This is a Biblical Kingdom principle.

Romans 4:17 says that you should call those things that are not as though they were. It describes how Abraham was promised a child at a ripe old age with a wife who was past child-bearing. But God began to challenge them to call those things that were not as though they were. Speak that you're going to have that child. You've got to call it, speak it, hear it, and believe it before you see it.

One classic illustration of the power of visualization is the story of Jacob's selective breeding of Laban's flock (See Genesis 30:37-42). Jacob asks Laban for his fair wages and Laban tries to shortchange him again. So, Jacob has a plan, "Listen. I will settle for all the speckled, spotted goats and the dark colored lambs." Laban agrees and, schemer that he is, takes away all of the spotted, speckled, dark colored flock to another place.

But God gave Jacob a creative strategy. It had to with visualization. Visualization is not only seeing it in your mind but setting visual things before you to help reinforce that mental picture.

*Jacob, however, took fresh-cut branches from poplar, almond and plane trees and made white stripes on them by peeling the bark and exposing the white inner wood of the branches. Then he placed the peeled branches in all the watering troughs, so that they would be directly in front of the flocks when they came to drink. When the flocks were in heat and came to drink, they mated in front of the branches. And they bore young that were streaked or speckled or spotted. Jacob set apart the young of the flock by themselves, but made the rest face the streaked and dark-colored animals that belonged to Laban. Thus he made separate flocks for himself and did not put them with Laban's animals. Whenever the stronger females were in heat, Jacob would place the branches in the troughs in front of the animals so they would mate near the branches, but if the animals were weak, he would not place them there. So the weak animals went to Laban and the strong ones to Jacob* (Genesis 30:37-42 NIV).

The problem with some of us is that we are not surrounding ourselves with enough visual cues to support our faith. Yes, you live by faith and not by sight but it's hard to keep living by faith when everything you see is a contradiction of what you believe in. You've got to surround yourself with people of similar faith as well as visual props. Make poster boards. If you are believing God for a house, then print that house out and put it on your vision or dream board. If you want a car, you put that car on there too. If you want a job, put that on as well. Whatever you are believing for you put it on the board. You march around and then you declare and decree that this is yours. You show it to the Lord and say, "Lord, look, here it is. This is what I want. This is what I want." Jacob placed visual props in front of the goats and sheep. As a result, they began to reproduce what they saw. The place of the visualization was where they began to conceive exactly there. If you want a college degree, you need to go visit a college. Go on a tour. If you want to have a certain type of job, a certain career, go around the people that have that career and ask them questions. If you're only acting based on what you have, then you are not positioning yourself for manifestation. Begin to act like where you want to go. Begin to surround yourself with where you want to be. You know some people say to fake it till you make it. That's not a Kingdom mindset. That's not the mentality that you want to have. You need to FAITH IT until it manifests. You're visualizing it. You're fighting for it until it manifests.

## Step Number Five: Make Space for Your Manifestation

Waiting for your manifestation is not a passive activity. As I mentioned before, that word waiting doesn't mean sitting around, twiddling your thumbs. When you speak the word of the Lord, you are working step five, which is making space for what you believe in to manifest.

You have to. This is a big thing that holds up so many people. You believe. You spoke that word. You know that it's in existence. It's hovering over where you sent it. You're doing your warfare. You're fighting devils. You're exercising your faith.

But you haven't made space for it to land. You can't believe God for $100,000 and you haven't even set up a bank account. Where are you going to put the money? You believe in God for a huge windfall but you don't even have a mechanism to accommodate what God brings to you. Why would God release the manifestation and there is nowhere for it to go? You've got to make space.

Look at 2 Kings 3:9-18. The kings of Israel, Judah and Edom are preparing for war against Moab. They are in the desert and they can't find any water for their troops and horses. King Jehoshaphat sends for the prophet Elisha and Elisha calls for a minstrel. As the minstrel plays music at the base, it stirs up the word of the Lord and he prophesies:

> *"Make this valley full of ditches. For thus says the Lord: 'You shall not see wind, nor shall you see rain; yet that valley shall be filled with water, so that you, your cattle, and your animals may drink.' And this is a simple matter in the sight of the Lord; He will also deliver the Moabites into your hand. Also you shall attack*

*every fortified city and every choice city, and shall cut down every good tree, and stop up every spring of water, and ruin every good piece of land with stones." Now it happened in the morning, when the grain offering was offered, that suddenly water came by way of Edom, and the land was filled with water* (See 2 Kings 3:9-20).

Notice, why did God require them to make ditches if not to contain the water He would supply? If there were no ditches to contain the water, there would be no use for it. Why would God supply what you're asking for it to be wasted, because you had not made appropriate accommodation for what you've been asking for?

You have a part to play at manifestation outside of having faith. You have to make space. The question is do you really understand what it takes to accommodate what you asked for? You spoke it. It's hovering, waiting for the time to land. The manifestation could be connected to your ability to accommodate. Could it be that your manifestation is delayed because you would not have the capacity to handle it when it came?

This is to challenge you, to motivate your faith, to speak in to you, and to stir you up to get busy really assessing what it's going to take to accommodate the manifestation and get busy by cooperating with God. Get ready today. Do not delay.

**Step Number Six: Break into Praise and Thanksgiving.**

When you begin to praise and thank God, it's a sign of faith. That's why it says, *"in everything give thanks; for this is the will of God in Christ Jesus for you"* (1 Thessalonians 5:18).

"In everything" implies even while you're waiting for manifestation.

You just need to thank God:

*I just thank you for my new house. I praise you, God, that the house is coming. It's going to look like this. Thank you for a house full of furniture. God, I just want to thank you for my new position. God, Thank you for my promotion. I just want you to praise You. You're so good. I thank you, God, that I'm above, I'm not beneath. God, I just want to praise You for what You're doing. Before You even do it, God, I want to praise You because it's already done in the spirit and I thank You for the manifestation, God.*

When you begin to praise God like that and begin to magnify and thank Him, you are accelerating the move of God in many ways. What would begin to happen is you position yourself for a victory with no sweat.

See what happened when King Jehoshaphat was threatened by three nations. But after the prophetic word came to tell him, *"The battle's not yours, it's the Lord's,"* he changed his strategy of conventional warfare to fight the battle the Lord's way.

*So they rose early in the morning and went out into the Wilderness of Tekoa; and as they went out, Jehoshaphat stood and said, "Hear me, O Judah and you inhabitants of Jerusalem: Believe in the Lord your God, and you shall be established; believe His prophets, and you shall prosper." And when he had consulted with the people, he appointed those who should sing to the Lord, and who should praise the beauty of holiness, as they went out before the army and were saying:*

*"Praise the Lord, For His mercy endures forever."*

*Now when they began to sing and to praise, the Lord set ambushes against the people of Ammon, Moab, and Mount Seir, who had come against Judah; and they were defeated. For the people of Ammon and Moab stood up against the inhabitants of Mount Seir to utterly kill and destroy them. And when they had made an end of the inhabitants of Seir, they helped to destroy one another* (2 Chronicles 20:20-23).

At God's command, the army were forth with worshippers and praisers leading the way. My God, he put worshippers and praisers, hallelujah, in front of the soldiers that they would praise the beauty of God's holiness! And they begin to say, "The Lord is good. His mercy endures for all generations."

How can you say the Lord is good when you have three kingdoms trying to come up against you all at once? It doesn't matter who comes up. There could be 20 people or 20 kingdoms coming up against you. But you know who your God is. He promised you protection. He promised you victory. He promised you deliverance. He said by the prophetic word that you would not have to fight but He was going to fight your battle for you.

Your sign of faith is to praise and thank Him. When the worshippers began to praise and thank God, He sent ambushes against the enemies to the point that the enemies began to attack themselves. When you began to praise and thank God in the midst of your enemies ready to overwhelm you, God would cause your enemies, the things that try to hold you up, and the things that try to fight your manifestation, to destroy themselves.

Praise is your weapon. It is also a sign of your faith and confidence in God. In the reality of the Kingdom the invisible word over your life is, in fact, true and it's only a matter of time before that thing comes to pass in the physical.

Some people are too dignified and too conscious of their self-importance to really stir up the praise that accelerates your manifestation. When you really need God to bring that thing on then, you've got to give God whole-hearted praise in an impossible situation.

# Appendix

5 Days of
Commanding Your Morning

# DAY 1:
# Four Winds

> *Read a chapter of Psalms and Proverbs*
> *(based on the day of the month)*
>
> *Listen to a song of worship and sing along*
>
> *Spend at least 15 minutes praying in the Spirit or praising God*

- Father in the name of Jesus, I thank you for a new day, new mercies, and new opportunities.

- I declare that this is the day that the LORD has made! I am rejoicing and I am exceedingly glad in it in Jesus' name.

- I declare and decree that I am seated in heavenly places therefore I am not praying earth-bound and have free course in the Spirit realm in Jesus' name.

- I command this day and take authority over every demonic force, scheme, or plans against me, my family, my destiny, and my day in the name of the Lord Jesus.

- I declare that the good, acceptable, and perfect will of God is my portion today in the name of Jesus Christ of Nazareth.

- I recognize that your Holy Spirit is with me and empowers me to see results in every aspect of my life.

- As Ezekiel called to the winds to bring life to the dead bones, I speak to the 4 winds to bring life to every dead thing in my life in Jesus' name.

- (FACE THE NORTH) Rise up, Oh LORD and let Your enemies be scattered. Let them that hate You flee before You. I prophesy to the North winds of promotion to blow in my life in Jesus' name.

- Promotion does not come from the East, the West, or the South. But you are the Judge! You set one up and you set one down!

- I declare that today I have been set up by you to be your ambassador in the sector you have assigned me to.

- (FACE THE EAST) Rise up, Oh LORD and let Your enemies be scattered. Let them that hate You flee before You. I prophesy to the East winds of protections to blow in my life protecting me from enemies and haters.

- I declare Psalms 91 in its entirety over me in Jesus' name! (Read Psalm 91 out loud)

- I declare that I dwell in the secret place of the Most High and abide under the feathers of the Almighty One.

- LORD you are my refuge and my fortress, in you alone I trust!

- I thank you God for exposing and removing all haters and enemies from my life in the name of the Lord Jesus!

- I declare and decree that as you did to Ahitophel, You would bring any information, wisdom, or strategies my haters and enemies have that could potential destroy me be brought to nothing in Jesus' name!

- I cancel and nullify every secret meeting, plan, and strategy against me, my family, and life in the name of Jesus Christ.

- I bless the nation of Israel, God's chosen people (both natural and spiritual), and pray for the peace and restoration of Jerusalem in the name of the Lord Jesus.

- (FACE THE SOUTH) Rise up, Oh LORD and let Your enemies be scattered. Let them that hate You flee before You. I prophesy to the South winds of supernatural provision to blow in my life.

- I stand on your promise that you have given your covenant people the power to get wealth for covenant building.

- Because I am a covenant person with a desire to establish your Kingdom on Earth, I pray for supernatural prosperity to be released in my life in Jesus' name.

- I declare and decree that I have multiple streams of incomes that flow out of my spiritual gifts, natural abilities, and acquired skills in the name of Jesus.

- I command unexpected finances to come to me today in Jesus' name!

- Raise up people and opportunities that will help me to increase in finances and influence in the name of the Lord Jesus.

- (FACE THE WEST) Rise up, Oh LORD and let Your enemies be scattered. Let them that hate You flee before You. I prophesy to the West winds of deliverance and healing to blow in my life.

- I rebuke any stronghold in my mind, heart, soul, and life now in Jesus' name.

- I declare and decree whom the Son has set free is free indeed. Therefore, I am free indeed in Jesus' name.

- I walk in total deliverance from every demonic force in Jesus' name.

- I claim full healing of my mind, body, and soul today in Jesus' name.

- By the stripes of Jesus, I have already been healed and I claim my healing now in Jesus' name.

- I repent of any actions that has given legal access to the enemy to bring sickness in my life and command that door to be closed now in Jesus' name.

- I declare and decree that I am child of God and healing is the children's bread. Therefore, I eat the bread of healing and receive immediate results in Jesus' name.

- (FACE ANY DIRECTION YOU WOULD LIKE) I seal this time of prayer in the name of the Lord Jesus and the blood of the Lamb, AMEN!

*End your time laying prostrate on your face or sit quietly for about 15 minutes so that you can hear what God has to say to you today. If you fall asleep, it is ok. Allow yourself to go.*

Good job Commander!!! Now you are ready to see manifestation in your day! Go rule for Christ in your world today!

# DAY 2:
# Prayers of Protection

> *Find a good devotional on your Bible app or a devotional book like Our Daily Bread*
>
> *Listen to a song of worship and sing along*
>
> *Spend at least 15 minutes praying in the Spirit or praising God*

- Good morning Father, Jesus, and Holy Spirit!
- Thank you for a new day that you foreordained before the Worlds begin.
- As I pray this morning, I get under the covering and protection of the early riser in Jesus' name.
- Your word says that those who seek you early will find you. Because I am up early, I declare and decree that I have unhindered audience with you and expect to see results today in Jesus' name.
- I thank you for your divine protection over my life. Your name oh Jehovah is a strong tower. I am righteous because of my faith in Jesus, thereby I run into your name and receive your protection.
- I command the morning to hear my voice and take hold of the ends of the Earth. Let the wicked be shaken out at my words in Jesus' name!
- I walk in my divine authority and treat upon the spirit of the serpent and declare that I cannot be harmed in Jesus' name.

- I am in your secret place and I am hidden under your shadow; therefore, I am untouchable by demonic powers in the name of the Lord Jesus.

- I pray for a divine hedge of protection to surround my family, my dreams, my purpose, my finances, my health, my mind, and everything concerning me in the name of the Lord Jesus.

- I repent for every word of perverseness that has created a breach in the spirit and ask that you seal up every opening in the hedge of my life in Jesus' name.

- I activate the five-fold protection that Job experience in my life:
    - I declare and decree that there is a hedge of protection around me;
    - A hedge around my household and family;
    - A hedge of protection around all my possessions;
    - And because of the hedge, the LORD blesses the works my hands; and
    - My possessions are increasing in the land in Jesus' name.

- I declare and decree in Jesus' name that NO WEAPON formed against me, my family, my health, my finances, my destiny, my relationships, my community, my nation, my church/ministry shall prosper in the name of the Lord Jesus.

- I refuse to be afraid of the arrow that flies by day or the terror that comes at night because I am covered by the Most High God.

- I command the strength of God inside of me to stand tall and prepare me to stand against the wiles of the enemy in Jesus' name.

- I put on the whole armor of God based upon Ephesians 6 in Jesus' name
    - My lions are gird with the belt of truth and I am living in God's truth in my inward being;
    - I have on the breastplate of righteousness and walk in right standing with God;
    - I put on the shoes of peace on my feet and carry the gospel of peace with me everywhere I go;
    - I take up the shield of faith and every fiery dart of the wicked one is totally blocked in my life;
    - I put the helmet of salvation on my head and declare that the mind that was in Christ Jesus is also operating in me. My mind is renewed and program in accordance with the word of God;
    - I am equipped with the sword of the Spirit, which is the word of God. The word is quick and powerful, sharper than a two-edged sword, cutting apart every opposition against my life;

- I pray without ceasing and I pray in the Spirit thereby confusing the enemy and directly communicating with my Father God in the name of Jesus.

- I enlist the assistance of Angels as God's messengers in my life today in the name of Jesus Christ.

- Angels, go to work on my behalf now and help me to be sensitive to your guidance in Jesus' name.

- I declare and decree that the chief Angel with his flaming swords is fighting on my behalf ahead of time thereby creating open passage for me in my day in Jesus' name.

- I bind every evil force that would attempt to capture my destiny and I loose the angelic assistance of God to bring my destiny to full manifestation in the name of Jesus Christ.

- I take out divine insurance on my movement, my family, and my possessions in Jesus' name.

- I declare and decree that revelations, healing, deliverance, breakthroughs, promotions, finances, relationships, requests in prayers, shifts, and transitions that have been demonically blocked or held up are being loosed unto me now in the name of the Lord Jesus.

- Every demonic agenda, evil thought pattern formed against the agenda of the Kingdom of God for my life is destroyed at the root by the fire of God in Jesus' name.

- I cover this prayer in the name of the Lord Jesus and in the blood of the Lamb! AMEN!

*End your time laying prostrate on your face or sit quietly for about 15 minutes so that you can hear what God has to say to you today. If you fall asleep, it is ok. Allow yourself to go.*

Good job Commander!!! Now you are ready to see manifestation in your day! Go rule for Christ in your world today!

# DAY 3:
## The Breaker's Anointing

> *Read a chapter of Psalms and Proverbs (based on the day of the month)*
>
> *Listen to a song of worship and sing along*
>
> *Spend at least 15 minutes praying in the Spirit or praising God*

- I thank you God for a fresh chance to experience life and your love today.

- I declare a new day, a new season, and a fresh anointing today in Jesus' name.

- I would have fainted if I did not believe to see your goodness in the land of the living. And because I am in the land of the living today, I declare and decree that I shall see and experience your goodness today in Jesus' name.

- May the goodness and favor of the Lord locate me and overtake me now in Jesus' name.

- I release the Breaker's anointing into my day and I declare and decree that there is no constriction, restriction, or limitation in my life in Jesus' name.

- I declare that every prison that I have been in has to let me go NOW in Jesus' name!

- I speak to every prison door and say be opened now and grant me free passage into deliverance now in the name of the Lord Jesus.

- I praise you God that I have been set free from the snare of the fowler in Jesus' name and my soul is now flying free as a bird in Jesus' name.

- I plead the blood of Jesus over demonic force at any level working against my life, my family, my purpose, my church, my city, and my nation in the name of the Lord Jesus.

- Every curse sent against my day is bound, broken, and rendered impotent now in Jesus' name.

- I release the Breaker's anointing to locate and destroy every dark altar, astral power, and satanic altar set against my destiny, prayers, and day in Jesus' name.

- I declare and decree that the Breaker's anointing will smash to pieces every demonic technology and device assigned against my progress and increase in the name of Jesus Christ.

- May the Breaker of the Lord locate and confound every enemy and hater that has purposed to oppose my day in Jesus' name.

- Let every stubborn pursue of my purpose and destiny be utterly destroyed in Jesus' name.

- I thank you Lord that because the Breaker of the Lord has been released into my day, every form of witchcraft, spells, occult work, or anything from the enemy that may be at work in my life is reversed and nullified in Jesus' name.

- Let every evil conspiracy that has formed against my life and destiny be disbanded and scattered now in Jesus' name.

- I release the spirit of deliverance to operate in every area of my life that is oppressed and under assault by the enemy in the name of Jesus Christ.

- I declare and decree that I have victory over my enemies every morning including today in the name of Jesus.

- I speak to this day, lift up your heads O ye gates and make way for the King of glory to come into through me in Jesus' name.

- I bind every destiny thief, destiny pirate, and destiny devourer in the name of Jesus. They are dethroned and rendered useless in the of the Lord Jesus.

- I walk in the divine dominion God has given me over all the elements and works of His hands in Jesus' name.

- I refuse to accept any and everything that is out of alignment with the word and promises of God. I stand against it now in Jesus' name and command it to conform to the will of God for me today in Jesus' name.

- I am confident that the Breaker's anointing is fully activated in my life and I am flowing in the good, acceptable, and perfect will of God for my life today in Jesus' name.

- I cover this prayer in the name of the Lord Jesus and the blood of the Lamb! AMEN!

*End your time laying prostrate on your face or sit quietly for about 15 minutes so that you can hear what God has to say to you today. If you fall asleep, it is ok. Allow yourself to go.*

Good job Commander!!! Now you are ready to see manifestation in your day! Go rule for Christ in your world today!

# DAY 4:
# Rebuking the Spirit of Pisgah

> *Find a good devotional on your Bible app or a devotional book like Our Daily Bread*
>
> *Listen to a song of worship and sing along*
>
> *Spend at least 15 minutes praying in the Spirit or praising God*

- God, I declare that today is the day that you have made! I am rejoicing and glad in it.

- I command the ears of the morning to hear my cry and respond favorably to me in the name of the Lord Jesus.

- I come into agreement with the Heavenlies and because of my agreement, Heaven is backing up my words and bring them into manifestation in Jesus' name.

- I declare and decree that today is my appointed time, my due season, and my day of manifestation in Jesus' name.

- Today is my receiving day in Jesus' name and I shall see results in my life today in Jesus' name.

- As the day breaks and my praise arises to you God, I declare and decree that the Earth shall yield increase to me in Jesus' name.

- I thank you that everything concerning me is in proper alignment in the name of Jesus.

- I declare and decree that I am strategically lined up with the ladder that touches the third Heaven and sits on the Earth in the name of the Lord Jesus.

- Because of my position, the angels are descending and ascending according to the words I speak in Jesus' name.

- I take my Kingdom authority and bind what is against the will of God for me and loose the good, acceptable, and perfect will of God in Jesus' name.

- I capture this day and declare that time is being redeemed for me today in Jesus' name.

- I recognize that there are some areas of my life that I have been going around the same mountain and not seeing results. Today, I call an end to that cycle in my life in Jesus' name.

- I refuse to come the edge of my promise and not cross over and possess in Jesus' name. I shall cross over successfully in Jesus' name.

- I rebuke and paralyze the spirit of Pisgah that allows me to come to the edge of the promise but not crossover and possess the promise in the name of the Lord Jesus.

- I declare and decree that I am going Northward into a posture of promotion and walking into what God says is mine today in Jesus' name.

- I repent for times in my past where I mishandled opportunities to bring glory to your name in people's lives in the name of Jesus Christ.

- I repent for walking in disobedience and not fully trusting You, especially in times of uncertainty. I declare that the I trust you like never before in Jesus' name.

- I come against all curses of leaking blessings in my life and I seal every breach in the name of Jesus.

- I remove my name from the book of seers of goodness without results in Jesus' name.

- God let me not put any unprofitable burdens on myself in Jesus' name.

- I declare and decree that the work of my hands and the sweat of my effort will not be in vain but will produce successful results in the name of Jesus.

- Let every power blocking me from receiving the good, acceptable, and perfect will of God be smashed by the hammer of the Lord, never to come together again in Jesus' name.

- I declare and decree that the lines, my portion are fallen on my behalf in pleasant, sweet, and agreeable places and I have a secure heritage in Jesus' name.

- I rebuke all anti-breakthrough and anti-miracle spirits designed against my life and command them to be shattered to pieces in the name of the Lord Jesus.

- Let the anointing to excel and prosper come greatly and mightily in every area of my life in the name of Jesus Christ.

- I receive the anointing to excel above my colleagues in the name of the Lord Jesus.

- By your Spirit, cause me to elevate into greatness for your glory in Jesus' name.

- I cover this time in prayer in the name of Jesus and the blood of the Lamb!

*End your time laying prostrate on your face or sit quietly for about 15 minutes so that you can hear what God has to say to you today. If you fall asleep, it is ok. Allow yourself to go.*

Good job Commander!!! Now you are ready to see manifestation in your day! Go rule for Christ in your world today!

# DAY 5:
## The Commander's Prayer

> *Read a few scriptures that encourage your spirit. Spend about 10 minutes thinking about what the passages mean to you at this time in your life, and then journal about it in a notebook.*
>
> *Listen to a song of worship and sing along*
>
> *Spend at least 15 minutes praying in the Spirit or praising God*

- Father in the name of Jesus, thank you for this brand new day you have given to me.

- I command this morning and take authority over it in Jesus' name.

- I command the cosmos to come into proper alignment with my divine purpose in Jesus' name.

- I speak to the sun, moon, and stars and command them to cooperate and facilitate God's purpose for my life in the name of Jesus.

- I thank you Lord that sun will not smite me by day nor the moon by night in Jesus' name

- I declare and decree that my sun and my moon is too hot to be handled, sat on, or moved in Jesus' name.

- I pray that any demonic or spiritual entity that tries to misalign me in the $1^{st}$ or $2^{nd}$ Heavenlies collide with the Ancient of Day, crash, burn, and die in the name of the Lord Jesus.

- I stand against every negative energy planning to operate against my life, family, or purpose today in Jesus' name.

- I dismantle any forces or powers uttering incantations against me to capture or lock up my days. I render it null and void in Jesus' name.

- I take hold of every stubborn problem in my life and I smash it against the Rock of my salvation and utterly destroy it in the name of Jesus.

- Because the LORD is with me, I declare and decree that I am possessing the gates of my enemies in Jesus' name.

- Let every evil conspirator gathering against me be disbanded and scattered by holy fire never to reconnect again in Jesus' name.

- I thank you that I have been created for a purpose and it has been destined that I shall do good in Jesus' name.

- I can never be thrown down or downgraded because I walk in the covenant favor of God.

- I declare and decree that I do not have poverty of body, soul, or spirit but I am overflowing in the name of Jesus.

- I renounce any unholy and ungodly covenants involving my life in Jesus' name.

- Anything that my ancestors have done on both sides of my family all the way back to Adam and Eve that has polluted my life, open the door to evil, or has caused curse to slow release in my life, be dismantled and nullified in my life now in Jesus' name.

- Lord please deliver me from what seems to be right but is actually wrong in Jesus' name.

- I come against every imagination and high thing that exalts itself against the knowledge of God.

- As I seek you and submit to your presence, I ask you to please reveal to me those things that give my enemies advantage over me in Jesus' name.

- I claim the victory of the cross of Calvary in the name of Jesus.

- I destroy every plan of satan that has formed against me in Jesus' name.

- I cast every form of witchcraft into darkness now in Jesus' name.

- Your word says you will not suffer a witch to live. I send back every evil work to its sender and I seal it in their head in the name of Jesus and the blood of the Lamb.

- I break every evil force siphoning my blessing with confusion and disorder in the name of Jesus.

- I rebuke every form of mental disorder and attack in my life in Jesus' name!

- I thank you Father for guarding my mind and heart against anxiety and depression with your peace that surpasses understanding in Jesus' name.

- Let the blood of Jesus poison the roots of all my problems and cause them to dry up and died in Jesus' name.

- I command healing to flow in my body now in Jesus' name.

- I reverse every improper operation of body organs or systems and command proper functioning now in the name of the Lord Jesus.

- By the stripes of Jesus, I have already been healed and I refuse to live in sickness in the name of Jesus Christ.

- Let the hunter of my health be redirected away from me now in Jesus' name.

- I declare that I am walking I prosperity and health even as my soul prospers in Jesus' name.

- I release financial overflow to manifest in my life in Jesus' name.

- I curse the root of any demonic force that causes me to remain in cycles of lack, debt, and poverty in Jesus' name.

- Let every dead area of my prosperity and purpose be resurrected by the Spirit of God in Jesus' name.

- May every embargo on my increase and success fall down and scatter now in the name of the Lord Jesus.

- I declare and decree that the hands of the Lord is greatly upon me and causes me to succeed in all I do in Jesus' name.

- I declare and decree that your favor is a shield around me and causes me to triumph over my enemy daily in Jesus' name.

- I walk daily in uncommon favor and God breaks rules for me that causes me to advance in every area of my life in the name of the Lord Jesus.

- Let the God of Abraham, Isaac, and Jacob manifest Yourself in Your covenant power to bless and prosper me in Jesus' name.

- Let every deep-rooted problem in my life dry up and be burned by the fire of God in the name of the Lord Jesus.

- I thank you God for downloading witty inventions, ideas, strategies, and plans to bring multiple streams of income into my life in Jesus' name.

- I call forth the right connections and opportunities to allow finances to flow into my life.

- I pray that former avenues of finances that have dried up in my life be reactivated and begin to flow again in the name of Jesus.

- I declare and decree that my angel of blessings will locate me every day of my life in Jesus' name.

- Lord God I pray that you would stretch your hand to perform signs and wonders in my life today in Jesus' name.

- I command the fire of God and the blood of Jesus to surround my purpose and destiny in Jesus' name.

- I walk in the authority and anointing that destroys every destiny killer in my life in the name of Jesus.

- I reclaim all of my departed glory and virtue to return to me now in double fold in Jesus' name.

- I praise you that you are recovering every stolen thing from me in the land of the living and dead and I receive total restoration in my life: nothing missing, nothing lacking, and nothing broken in Jesus' name!

- Jesus, I thank you for the victory today!

- I announce that my name is written in the Lamb's book of life and cannot be erased in Jesus' name.

- I seal this prayer in the name of the Lord Jesus and by the blood of the Lamb!! AMEN!

*End your time laying prostrate on your face or sit quietly for about 15 minutes so that you can hear what God has to say to you today. If you fall asleep, it is ok. Allow yourself to go.*

Good job Commander!!! Now you are ready to see manifestation in your day! Go rule for Christ in your world today!

# ABOUT THE AUTHOR

A native of Atlanta, Georgia, Dr. David E. Jackson is a highly sought-after speaker, life coach, and consultant throughout the United States, Africa, and the Caribbean. Dr. Jackson is the Lead Pastor of The Rock ATL International Fellowship (www.therockatl.org), an Assemblies of God church with a vision to release Kingdom influencers into every sector. The Rock ATL is one of the fastest growing congregations in the city of College Park and since its inception in 2018, has impacted its community through outreach, discipleship, fellowship, and strategic partnerships. Dr. Jackson is a consecrated Bishop in the Light of the World Covenant Fellowship based in Stockbridge, GA with an international adherence of over 250,000 people.

In the marketplace, Dr. Jackson is a Curriculum Writer and Trainer at the Jack McDowell School for Leadership Development at the Salvation Army-Evangeline Booth College in Atlanta, GA. In addition, Dr. Jackson is the CEO of D. E. Jackson Enterprises, LLC: a coaching, ministry, and consulting firm. He is a former police officer and senior instructor with the Atlanta Police Department, has served as a chief-of-staff in the New York City Council, and worked in the non-profit sector. His previous work has afforded him extensive national and international travel including travel to over 15 nations.

Dr. Jackson believes firmly in education and self-development. He received his B.A. from Cornell University; MDiv. from Union Theological Seminary of New York; and DMin. from the New York Theological Seminary. He is currently a PhD student at Southeastern University studying Organizational Leadership.

Dr. Jackson is the recipient of several awards and honors including the Presidential Lifetime Achievement Award, Fund for Theological Education (FTE) Fellow, the Maxwell Fellowship for Promise to Parish Ministry, and an honorary doctorate in Humanitarian. He is a proud member of Alpha Phi Alpha Fraternity, Inc., Crisis Intervention Trainers International, and the African American Leadership for the Philos Project. He is an alumnus of the North Carolina Outward Bound Outdoors Educational School and resides in South Fulton, GA.

## CONTACT INFORMATION
Dr. David E. Jackson
D.E. Jackson Enterprises, LLC
3645 Marketplace Blvd, Ste. 130-266
East Point, GA 30344
770-231-5431
dejacksonenterprises@gmail.com
www.dejackson.org

www.ingramcontent.com/pod-product-compliance
Lightning Source LLC
Chambersburg PA
CBHW071002080526
44587CB00015B/2315